# Research and Resources in Support of *This We Believe*

Research Committee, National Middle School Association

Vincent A. Anfara, Jr., Contributing Editor
P. Gayle Andrews
David L. Hough
Steven B. Mertens
Nancy B. Mizelle
George P. White

**National Middle School Association
Westerville, Ohio**

National Middle School Association
4151 Executive Parkway, Suite 300
Westerville, Ohio 43081
Telephone: (800) 528-NMSA
www.nmsa.org

**NMSA**

Printed in the United States of America.

Sue Swaim, Executive Director
Jeff Ward, Associate Executive Director
Edward Brazee, Editor, Professional Publications
John Lounsbury, Consulting Editor, Professional Publications
April Tibbles, Director of Publications
Mary Mitchell, Designer, Editorial Assistant
Dawn Williams, Production Specialist
Mark Shumaker, Graphic Designer
Marcia Meade-Hurst, Senior Publications Representative

**Library of Congress Cataloging-in-Publication Data**
Research and resources in support of This we believe/ by Research Committee, National Middle School Association; Vincent A. Anfara, Jr., contributing editor, and P. Gayle Andrews ... [et al.].
   p. cm.
  Includes bibliographical references.
  ISBN 1-56090-143-8 (pbk.)
   1. Middle schools--United States. 2. Middle schools--Research--United States. I. Anfara, Vincent A. II. Andrews, P. Gayle, date III. National Middle School Association. Research Committee. IV. This we believe.

LB1623.5.R46 2003
373.2'36--dc22

                                             2003044273

Today, with new intensity, educators, researchers, parents, and policy-makers are working to create successful schools for young adolescents. In collaboration they are searching to blend philosophy and practice based upon sound research that will result in a quality educational experience for every 10- to 15-year-old.

As a part of National Middle School Association's commitment to this cause, we are pleased to present *Research and Resources in Support of This We Believe,* a companion document to NMSA's position paper, *This We Believe: Successful Schools for Young Adolescents.* This document for the first time brings together research studies and related resources that support sound educational practices for young adolescents.

Together these two significant documents provide the philosophy, practice, and research needed to guide the implementation of successful middle level schools. Educators, parents, and policymakers must work in concert in their own communities to apply these principles and practices. However, they should do so with the clear knowledge that the middle level concept, when implemented consistently over time, results in higher academic achievement while effectively meeting the other developmental needs of these young adolescents. It is also important to keep in mind these words from the position paper: "Schools should not choose among characteristics, implementing only those that appear to be more achievable or seem more appropriate for a particular situation. Rather, successful middle level schools recognize that the 14 characteristics described are interdependent and must be implemented in concert."

A special thanks goes to Vincent A. Anfara, Jr., P. Gayle Andrews, David L. Hough, Steven B. Mertens, Nancy B. Mizelle, and George P. White, members of National Middle School Association's Research Committee. These individuals worked diligently to identify the research studies and resources that comprise this document. Vincent Anfara deserves special recognition for his leadership in bringing this major project to completion.

Sue Swaim, Executive Director
National Middle School Association

# National Middle School Association
# Research Committee

**George P. White,** Committee Chair, and Professor of Education and Human Services, Lehigh University, Bethlehem, Pennsylvania

**P. Gayle Andrews,** Assistant Professor of Middle School Education, The University of Georgia, Athens

**Vincent A. Anfara, Jr.,** Associate Professor of Educational Administration and Policy Studies, University of Tennessee, Knoxville

**David L. Hough,** Dean, College of Education and Professor of Research and Statistics, Southwest Missouri State University, Springfield

**Steven B. Mertens,** Senior Research Scientist, The Center for Prevention Research and Development, University of Illinois, Champaign

**Nancy B. Mizelle,** Assistant Professor of Middle Grades Education, Georgia College & State University, Milledgeville

# Contents

# Preface

*Research and Resources in Support of This We Believe* was developed as a companion volume to *This We Believe: Successful Schools for Young Adolescents* (National Middle School Association, 2003). As such it is not meant to be read from cover to cover, but instead is to be used as a tool in creating successful middle schools. It is our hope that the research summarized and documented in this book will assist middle level practitioners and policymakers in adopting and implementing sound educational practices for young adolescents.

*Research and Resources* is divided into five major parts. Part One, Introduction, provides the reader with the rationale for this book and an overview of middle level research that has occurred since 1991. Part Two reviews the major studies that have grounded and helped to conceptualize *This We Believe* (National Middle School Association, 1995) and *Turning Points* (Carnegie Council on Adolescent Development, 1989) as integrated reform initiatives. In this part we focus on research that specifically links the middle school concept to improved student academic performance and social-emotional development. Part Three reviews the research that has been conducted on each of the six programmatic components of *This We Believe: Successful Schools for Young Adolescents*. Part Four addresses the need for middle level teachers and administrators who are specifically prepared to work in middle schools. In Parts Three and Four we provide readers not only with research summaries but with annotated references and recommended resources. The annotated references include important research that has been conducted and is worthy of further investigation and in-depth reading. The recommended resources, while based somewhat on research, are more practical in nature and provide examples of the *This We Believe* programmatic components in action. Finally, Part Five, Directions for Future Research, presents a preview of the next steps that are necessary to build a solid foundation for the middle school concept.

...

PART ONE

# Introduction

***This We Believe: Successful Schools for Young Adolescents*** (National Middle School Association, 2003) presents a philosophical or conceptual framework to guide the development of school programs that effectively serve the needs of young adolescents. The primary question that educators, parents, and policymakers have about the middle school is "Does it work?" or "Will this model result in higher achievement while meeting other developmental needs of young adolescents as well?" The myth that middle schools are "too soft" and lack academic rigor persists, and many in the general public so believe, in spite of evidence to the contrary. We need to debunk this myth about middle schools. This is possible with the results of research studies combined with cumulative experience. What, then, do we really know about the effectiveness of middle level education? What kinds of schools are best for young adolescents? Is there research to support the type of school proposed in the position paper?

This companion volume, *Research and Resources in Support of This We Believe,* addresses these questions and presents summaries of research on the programmatic components described in *This We Believe: Successful Schools for Young Adolescents* (NMSA, 2003). It provides educators and policymakers with a considerable understanding of what is currently known about middle level practice. To facilitate ongoing discussions, planning, and policy development at the local level, annotated references and recommended resources are also included.

## Developing an operational definition of "research"

Much has been published on middle schools. For every serious research study a number of opinion pieces exist on a wide variety of middle level topics. In response, we modified Hough's (2003) definition to guide the selection of sources to be included in *Research and Resources in Support of This We Believe.*

> **Research is an original work that reports the methods**
> **and findings from the systematic collection and analysis**
> **of empirical data.**

Using this operational definition, we were able to include reviews of literature or conceptual pieces that utilized others' works, provided these stand-alone documents did, in fact, use systematic approaches and follow standard scientific steps for data collection and analysis. Applying this definition, we included some "research" that would not have been labeled as such by those engaged in experimental research.

## An overview of middle level education research, 1991-2002

Between 1991 and 2002, 3,717 studies related to middle schools were published. That is an average of 309 per year over a 12-year period of time, almost one published study per day. This accounts only for the research that Hough and his research team (2003) identified.

While dissertations account for a large portion of this research (just under one-half), documents and journal articles indexed in ERIC (Educational Resources Information Center) account for two-thirds of all the studies disseminated. The American Educational Research Association (AERA) is the leading organization disseminating middle level education research, followed by National Middle School Association. Research on middle level topics peaked in 1998 when almost 12 percent of the total number of studies were disseminated, and by 2002 the volume of research had receded to roughly six percent or half that of 1998 (Hough, 2003).

Surprisingly, many topics identified in *The 21st Century Research Agenda: Issues, Topics & Questions Guiding Inquiry into Middle Level Theory*

*& Practice* (NMSA, 1997) and the corresponding programmatic character-istics and structures found in *This We Believe* (NMSA, 1995) have not been adequately addressed in the research, including flexible scheduling, adult ad-vocates for students, school climate, and health and wellness issues (Hough, 2003).

About two-thirds of all studies on middle level education are qualita-tive in nature and have become increasingly so over the past 12 years, while quantitative studies that once represented almost 30 percent of the total now represent about 15 percent. The data collection techniques of choice among researchers conducting middle level education research include unobtrusive methods, case studies, and mixed approaches. Less common are observa-tion, surveys, and interviews. Meta-analyses and focus groups are few and far between. Few experimental designs have been conducted, under four per-cent of the total of 3,717 studies. Action research accounts for approximately 20 percent of the studies and has grown exponentially as a method of choice (Hough, 2003).

Universities support almost 90 percent of all middle level research con-ducted. The leading institutions providing this support are, in order: The University of Georgia, Columbia University's Teachers College, University of South Carolina, University of Nebraska-Lincoln, and (tied for fifth) Ohio State University, Temple University, and the University of Alabama (Hough, 2003).

Hough (2003) found that over 90 percent of the research has been con-ducted by individuals not identified as prominent middle school advocates. One finding we stumbled upon serendipitously was that virtually no middle level education studies were replications of prior efforts. That is, no one has used the same research design and methods to collect, analyze, and report findings that another researcher had employed. Replicating studies is a must if the research base is to be validated. Medical research, for example, is filled with replications to validate previous findings.

## The need for additional research

The landscape of middle level research is painted using many different brushes and diverse styles, so the resulting product is somewhat confusing. But, as mentioned earlier, there is an urgency regarding research in this area. Acknowledging this urgency, Felner and associates (1997) wrote, "Although a more well-developed research base does not, by itself, ensure more successful reform efforts, without such a foundation the progress and fruits of reform efforts will continue to be disappointing" (p. 41).

The inconclusive nature of the findings related to the effects of middle school practices on student achievement has been documented (see *NMSA Research Summary #12: Academic Achievement,* 2001; Brown, Roney, & Anfara, 2003; Van Zandt & Totten, 1995). But this is not unusual in the realm of educational research. Reviewing the literature on many different educational topics reveals research that supports, negates, or shows no difference in the relationship among the variables being studied. However, the inconclusive nature of middle school research should not be adopted as a rationale for inaction or refusal to move forward in improving middle level schools. There is, indeed, a promising and expanding body of research that demonstrates positive results when schools fully implement the recommended tenets of the middle school philosophy.

References Cited

Brown, K. M., Roney, K., & Anfara, Jr., V. A. (2003). Organizational health directly influences student performance at the middle level. *Middle School Journal, 34*(5), 5-15.

Felner, R., Jackson, A., Kasak, D., Mulhall, P., Brand, S., & Flowers, N. (1997). The impact of school reform for the middle grades: A longitudinal study of a network engaged in Turning Points-based comprehensive school transformation. In R. Takanishi & D. A. Hamburg (Eds.), *Preparing adolescents for the twenty-first century: Challenges facing Europe and the United States* (pp. 38-69). Cambridge, UK: Cambridge University Press.

Hough, D. L. (2003). *R3=Research, rhetoric, and reality: A study of studies addressing NMSA's 21st Century Research Agenda and This We Believe.* Westerville, OH: National Middle School Association.

National Middle School Association. (1995). *This we believe: Developmentally responsive middle level schools.* Columbus, OH: Author.

National Middle School Association. (1997). *A 21st century research agenda: Issues, topics & questions guiding inquiry into middle level theory & practice.* Columbus, OH: Author.

National Middle School Association. (2001). *NMSA research summary #12: Academic achievement.* Retrieved July 24, 2003, from http://www.nmsa.org

National Middle School Association. (2003). *This we believe: Successful schools for young adolescents.* Westerville, OH: Author..

Van Zandt, L. M., & Totten, S. (1995). The current status of middle level education research: A critical review. *Research in Middle Level Education Quarterly, 18*(3), 1-25.

PART TWO

# Research That Looks at the Middle School Concept as an Integrated Reform Model

F our major studies examined the middle school concept as an integrated reform model and its effects on student academic and social-emotional performance. These studies include research conducted by Lee and Smith (1993), Felner et al. (1997), Mertens, Flowers, and Mulhall (1998), and Backes, Ralston, and Ingwalson (1999).

In 1993 Lee and Smith evaluated how middle school policies and practices influenced the students who attend them, focusing specifically on achievement, engagement, and equity issues. The sample for this study was drawn from the *National Education Longitudinal Study of 1988* (NELS:88). Because of the nature of this database Lee and Smith acknowledged that they are "not sure whether the sample of students in schools that reported that they engage in practices like heterogeneous grouping and team teaching actually encountered instruction in this way" (p. 180). Neither did they know the level of implementation of these practices. Specifically they looked at reduced departmentalization, heterogeneous grouping, and team teaching as a "composite measure" of restructured middle schools.

Lee and Smith's (1993) findings indicated that the elements of restructuring were positively associated with academic achievement and engagement with schooling of eighth graders. Students who attended schools that encourage team teaching evidenced higher achievement. Additionally, less grouping by ability and a less rigid departmental structure appeared to promote social equity in achievement among students. In relation to engagement, Lee and Smith found that "although attending restructured schools may positively influence academic engagement, this engagement may coexist with higher levels of at-risk behaviors" (p. 180).

Felner and his associates (1997) conducted significant and compelling research that acknowledges the necessity of implementing Turning Points' recommendations as a comprehensive reform initiative. This team of researchers studied a network of 31 Illinois middle schools during the 1991-1992 school year. These schools represented a range of geographic, demographic, and size characteristics, including rural, suburban, and urban schools.

Felner's group (1997) sought to "assess and evaluate the process of implementation of the recommendations of Turning Points for middle grades reform, as well as their impact on students' academic achievement, social-emotional development, and behavioral adjustment" (p. 42). Of particular concern was the association between the levels of implementation of the reform that participating schools attained and relevant student outcomes. The researchers obtained data on sets of schools that were at different levels of maturity (high, partial, or low) in reform implementation. The primary source of data was a set of annual surveys, the *High Performance Learning Communities Assessments* (HiPLaCes-A). These surveys were administered to teachers, staff members, students, administrators, and selected parents. Additional data were obtained from student records, attendance, and scores (reading, mathematics, and language arts) on local and state achievement tests.

Results of this longitudinal study indicated, "...across subject areas, adolescents in highly implemented schools had higher achievement (as measured by the Iowa Test of Basic Skills and the California Test of Basic Skills) than those in nonimplemented schools and substantially better than those in partially implemented schools" (p. 55). Felner and associates (1997) concluded, "...broad-range enhancements and adjustment are not obtained until implementation is quite mature, comprehensive, and conducted with a high degree of fidelity" (p. 67).

Researchers at the Center for Prevention Research and Development (CPRD) looked at 155 Michigan middle schools that participated in the Michigan Middle Start Initiative funded in 1994 by the W. K. Kellogg Foundation. Surveys (the School Improvement Self-Study) were administered to principals, teachers, and students in 1994-95 and in 1996-97 by the Center for Prevention Research and Development. This self-study uses 24 scales to measure progress in dimensions of reform including curriculum, school climate, instruction, family involvement, professional development, and school organization.

Specifically, Mertens, Flowers, and Mulhall (1998) focused on trends related to teaching practices and learning environments and their relationship to student achievement, behaviors, and attitudes. By design the researchers compared and contrasted the progress of two groups of Middle Start schools: grant schools and non-grant schools. The "grant" schools group consisted of 21 schools that received intensive comprehensive school reform services, including individual school grants, on-site technical assistance, professional development, and networking opportunities. The "non-grant" group contained 134 schools that participated in the self-study but did not receive any other school reform services. Their findings indicate that the 21 Middle Start grant schools improved in both reading and math achievement scores over the two-year period, as measured by the Michigan Educational Assessment Program (MEAP). "Compared to the non-grant schools, the Middle Start grant schools showed dramatic gains in both seventh grade reading (+10 %) and math (+6 %) MEAP scores from 1994-95 to 1996-97" (p. 92).

Students reported higher levels of stress to succeed academically but felt safer at their schools in 1996-97 than they did in 1994-95. Additionally, Middle Start grant schools displayed several positive improvements in the areas of student adjustment, behavior, and substance use (a decrease in the reported use of alcohol). Students reported more positive self-esteem and academic efficacy. Lastly, teachers reported working more effectively to serve the needs of early adolescents and having more contact with parents and guardians. Schools implementing the Middle Start Initiative are showing improved capacity for continuous improvement.

CPRD is also a partner in this project's expansion with the Foundation for the Mid-South's Middle Start Initiative. Middle schools in Louisiana, Arkansas, and Mississippi began participating in this project in 1998. In the area of academic achievement, the Arkansas Middle Start schools (80 schools) scored slightly higher on the 1998 reading and language achievement tests (SAT9) than the state-wide group of middle level schools (Center for Prevention Research and Development, 1999a). In Louisiana, Middle Start schools (68 schools) scored about the same on ITBS achievement tests as the state-wide group of middle schools (CPRD, 1999b). Mississippi Middle Start schools (67 schools) had slightly higher student achievement scores (CTBS/5) in language arts, reading, and mathematics as compared to the state-wide group of middle level schools (CPRD, 1999c). In short, these findings seem to suggest that Middle Start schools, despite their higher percentages of economically disadvantaged students, are keeping pace with the state averages (state averages include a higher percentage of more affluent schools).

Finally in 1999, Backes, Ralston, and Ingwalson examined the impact of middle school practices on student achievement in North Dakota's Middle Grade School State Policy Initiative (MGSSPI) schools, called BRIDGES schools. The major question asked was, "What effect has the implementation of middle level practices by BRIDGES Project schools had on student achievement in grades six though eight compared to non-BRIDGES schools in North Dakota?" The authors of this study admit that they "…assumed that each of the recommended middle school practices had been implemented, [and] that students in BRIDGES Project systemic change schools should have measurable gains in student achievement because of the implementation of these practices…" (p. 49).

The findings of the Backes, Ralston, and Ingwalson (1999) study indicated that the composite grade equivalent score from grades six to eight was higher in BRIDGES Project schools than in non-BRIDGES schools in the areas of reading vocabulary, language mechanics, study skills, science, and social studies. There was no difference in composite grade equivalent scores in reading comprehension and spelling. Non-BRIDGES students outperformed BRIDGES students in the areas of language expression, math computation, and math concepts and applications.

The results of these four studies are promising. They provide middle level practitioners, scholars, advocates, and policymakers with a firm foundation that links the middle school concept to improved student academic and social-emotional development. These studies also provide a point of departure for the design and conduct of future research. In 1995 Van Zandt and Totten concluded that middle school research included an insufficient number of studies, weak research designs, difficulties comparing studies with conflicting designs, and too little attention to the effects of extraneous variables (i.e., socioeconomic status) on outcomes. While three of the four studies reported here were conducted since 1995 more research is needed.

## References Cited

Backes, J., Ralston, A., & Ingwalson, G. (1999). Middle level reform: The impact on student achievement. *Research in Middle Level Education Quarterly, 22*(3), 43-57.

Center for Prevention Research and Development. (1999a, September). *1998/99 Arkansas Middle Start: An executive summary.* Champaign, IL: Author. Retrieved July 24, 2003, from http://www.cprd.uiuc.edu

Center for Prevention Research and Development. (1999b, September). *1998/99 Louisiana Middle Start: An executive summary.* Champaign, IL: Author. Retrieved July 24, 2003, from http://www.cprd.uiuc.edu

Center for Prevention Research and Development. (1999c, September). *1998/99 Mississippi Middle Start: An executive summary.* Champaign, IL: Author. Retrieved July 24, 2003, from http://www.cprd.uiuc.edu

Felner, R., Jackson, A., Kasak, D., Mulhall, P., Brand, S., & Flowers, N. (1997). The impact of school reform for the middle grades: A longitudinal study of a network engaged in Turning Points-based comprehensive school transformation. In R. Takanishi & D. A. Hamburg (Eds.), *Preparing adolescents for the twenty-first century: Challenges facing Europe and the United States* (pp. 38-69). Cambridge, UK: Cambridge University Press.

Lee, V. E., & Smith, J. B. (1993). Effects of school restructuring on the achievement and engagement of middle-grade students. *Sociology of Education, 66*(3), 164-187.

Mertens, S. B., Flowers, N., & Mulhall, P. (1998). *The Middle Start Initiative, phase 1: A longitudinal analysis of Michigan middle-level schools.* (A report to the W. K. Kellogg Foundation). Urbana, IL: University of Illinois. Retrieved July 24, 2003, from http://www.cprd.uiuc.edu

National Center for Education Statistics. (1988). *National educational longitudinal study of 1988.* Washington, DC: U. S. Department of Education.

Van Zandt, L. M., & Totten, S. (1995). The current status of middle level education research: A critical review. *Research in Middle Level Education Quarterly, 18*(3), 1-25.

PART THREE

# Research on This We Believe
# Programmatic Components

In *This We Believe: Successful Schools for Young Adolescents* (2003), National Middle School Association identifies six components that successful middle schools should provide for the education of young adolescents. These programmatic components are

(1) Curriculum that is relevant, challenging, integrative, and exploratory

(2) Multiple learning and teaching approaches that respond to their diversity

(3) Assessment and evaluation programs that promote quality learning

(4) Organizational structures that support meaningful relationships and learning

(5) School-wide efforts and policies that foster health, wellness, and safety

(6) Multifaceted guidance and support services.

In Part Three we give a brief summary of research related to the programmatic components of exemplary middle schools and provide annotated summaries of related research along with a list of recommended resources for use in implementing these components.

# 1. CURRICULUM THAT IS RELEVANT, CHALLENGING, INTEGRATIVE, AND EXPLORATORY.

## Research Summary

In *This We Believe: Successful Schools for Young Adolescents* (National Middle School Association, 2003), curriculum is said to encompass "every planned aspect of a school's education program," from the skills and knowledge addressed within specific classes to school services and various student activities. Within this comprehensive definition, effective curriculum for young adolescents should be relevant, challenging, integrative, and exploratory.

*(1) To be relevant,* curriculum must give students the opportunity to explore questions and concerns related to themselves and the world around them. Haberman (1991) offers several indicators of a relevant curriculum including students' studying issues they regard as critical and focusing on concepts instead of isolated facts. The ground-breaking research report, *How People Learn* contends that experts organize their knowledge around important concepts, the big ideas (Bransford, Brown, & Cocking, 1999). A relevant curriculum moves beyond isolated facts and analyzes those big ideas in depth, helping students ground the conceptual understanding they will need to answer the ultimate question about relevance, "Why do we need to know this?"

*(2) To be challenging,* curriculum must engage students in active learning that stretches their capacities to acquire vital, relevant knowledge and skills and allows them to gradually assume control over their own learning. Middle level educators continue their efforts to stretch every student's capacity in classrooms containing students of diverse ability and achievement levels, as the evidence about tracking's "inherent inequity and ineffectiveness" (Jackson & Davis, 2000, p. 67) continues to grow (Braddock & Slavin, 1992; Gamoran, Nystrand, Berends, & LePorte, 1995; Oakes, Gamoran, & Page, 1992; Wheelock, 1992). To enhance their motivation and stretch their growing sense of autonomy, students, particularly at-risk students, must have re-

sponsibility and choices related to their own learning (Baker, 1996; Benard, 1993; Haberman, 1991; Higgs & Tarsi, 1997).

*(3) To be integrative,* curriculum must connect learning to students' lives, provide opportunities to reflect, and foster students' application of their emerging intellectual, social, physical, and technological skills to substantive problems and issues. According to Nesin (2000), when curriculum is integrative, "Students gain knowledge from mandated curriculum and from a variety of other sources, questioning and synthesizing all sources and evolving a new body of knowledge from the combination. The design unifies diverse young people toward common goals, forming a caring democratic community and preparing students to participate in a diverse democratic society" (p. 39). Beane (1997) believes that, by definition, curriculum integration must involve students' voices and choices.

*(4) To be exploratory,* curriculum must offer experiences students can use to discover their own talents and preferences, to make contributions to their communities, and to become familiar with hobbies and interests they may want to pursue for a lifetime. Rogers and Freiberg (1994) describe learning as a continuum, with the learning of isolated facts at one end and "significant, meaningful, experiential learning" at the other (p. 36). The latter kind of learning "has a strong component of self-discovery...real life experience, the coming together of the cognitive and the affective, and the appeal to natural curiosity" (Daniels & Bizar, 1998, p. 170). Students' questions, talents, concerns about themselves and their communities, and their interests can form the basis for exploration that takes them beyond what they know to the previously unimagined.

In practice, all the elements of an effective curriculum for young adolescents intertwine. Relevance, challenge, integration, and exploration each support and reinforce strong connections between schooling and each and every middle grades student.

## References Cited

Baker, A. (1996). Major disciplinary violations in junior high school: An explanatory study. *Research in Middle Level Education Quarterly, 19*(3), 1-20.

Beane, J. (1997). *Curriculum integration: Designing the core of democratic education.* New York: Teachers College Press.

Benard, B. (1993). Fostering resiliency in kids. *Educational Leadership, 51*(3), 44-48.

Braddock, J. H., II, & Slavin, R. E. (1992, September). *Why ability grouping must end: Achieving excellence and equity in American education.* Center for Research on Effective Schooling for Disadvantaged Students, Johns Hopkins University. Paper presented at the Common Destiny Conference, Washington, DC.

Bransford, J. D., Brown, A. L., & Cocking, R. R. (Eds.). (1999). *How people learn: Brain, mind, experience, and school.* Washington, DC: National Academy Press.

Daniels, H., & Bizar, M. (1998). *Methods that matter: Six structures for best practice classrooms.* Portland, ME: Stenhouse.

Gamoran, A., Nystrand, M., Berends, M., & Le Porte, P. (1995). An organizational analysis of the effects of ability grouping. *American Educational Research Association Journal, 32*(4), 687-715.

Haberman, M. (1991). The pedagogy of poverty versus good teaching. *Phi Delta Kappan, 73*(4), 290-294.

Higgs, G. E., & Tarsi, N. L. (1997). New learning and agency in the at-promise student. In R. F. Kronick (Ed.), *At-risk youth: Theory, practice and reform* (pp. 78-92). New York: Garland Publishing.

Jackson, A. W., & Davis, G. A. (2000). *Turning points 2000: Educating adolescents in the 21st century.* New York: Teachers College Press.

National Middle School Association. (2003). *This we believe: Successful schools for young adolescents.* Westerville, OH: Author.

Nesin, G. (2000). *Young adolescent achievement and attitudes in various curriculum designs.* Unpublished doctoral dissertation, The University of Georgia, Athens.

Oakes, J., Gamoran, A., & Page, R. N. (1992). Curriculum differentiation: Opportunities, outcomes, and meanings. In P. W. Jackson (Ed.), *Handbook of research on curriculum* (pp. 570-608). New York: Macmillan.

Rogers, C., & Freiberg, H. J. (1994). *Freedom to learn.* New York: Macmillan.

Wheelock, A. (1992). *Crossing the tracks: How "untracking" can save America's schools.* New York: The New Press.

## Annotated References

Beane, J. (1997). *Curriculum integration: Designing the core of democratic education.* New York: Teachers College Press.

In this critical resource on curriculum integration, Beane highlights classroom examples that demonstrate the power and potential of curriculum developed collaboratively by students and teachers and organized around social issues and students' personal experiences and concerns, without regard for subject-area boundaries. In research grounded in historical, philosophical, and qualitative inquiry, Beane outlines how and why this curriculum design theory works. To remove the "fad" tag too often associated with it, he traces curriculum integration's roots to the 19th century. To provide a sense of what it looks and sounds like, he describes the questions students ask about themselves and the world, the processes students and teachers together have developed for tackling those questions, and the connections students and teachers have made between their learning and the content standards required by schools and districts. Finally, he acknowledges the reality of curriculum integration in a nation focused on standards and standardized tests, and finds reasons for hope in the work of educators across the country collaborating with their students to learn democratically.

Bransford, J. D., Brown, A. L., & Cocking, R. R. (Eds.). (1999). *How people learn: Brain, mind, experience, and school.* Washington, DC: National Academy Press.

For two years, the National Research Council's Committee on Developments in the Science of Learning reviewed advances in the science of learning from multiple fields of study including cognitive psychology, neuroscience, human development, social psychology, education, and anthropology. The committee's final report, *How People Learn*, synthesizes key research findings from hundreds of research studies within a framework focused on learners and learning and teachers and teaching. The implications for educators are substantial and varied, with follow-up publications forthcoming (e.g., *How Students Learn: History, Math, and Science in the Classroom*) that will spell out those implications in even more detail.

Lipka, R., Lounsbury, J., Toepfer, C., Vars, G., Alessi, S., & Kridel, C. (1998). *The Eight-Year Study revisited: Lessons from the past for the present.* Columbus, OH: National Middle School Association.

A reconsideration of the most extensive research study on curriculum ever conducted, this book is one that all middle school leaders should study carefully. The findings of *The Eight-Year Study*, released in 1942 but never widely distributed, deserve thoughtful attention. The most important aspects of this study are reviewed, a discussion of how 30 schools across the country successfully broke from traditional curriculum approaches is presented, and implications for present curriculum work are addressed.

Lounsbury, J., & Marani, J. (1964). *The junior high school we saw: One day in the eighth grade.* Alexandria, VA: Association of Supervision and Curriculum Development; Lounsbury, J., Marani, J., & Compton, M. (1980). *The middle school in profile: A day in the seventh grade.* Columbus, OH: National Middle School Association; Lounsbury, J., & Johnston, H. (1985). *How fares the ninth grade?* Lounsbury, J., & Johnston, H. (1988). *Life in the three sixth grades.* Lounsbury, J., & Clark, D. (1990). *Inside grade eight: From apathy to excitement.* Reston, VA: National Association of Secondary School Principals.

The above five studies of middle level grades conducted on a national level provide a realistic and revealing look at what students actually experience in school. In all of the studies, volunteer observers shadowed randomly selected students on the same day in various states across the country, recording at five to seven minute intervals what that individual student was doing or experiencing. At the end of the day, the observer interviewed the student to secure responses on several questions. Packets of about 20 observation forms minus the observer's personal reflections were sent to analysts. Out of these very dramatic glimpses of education from the standpoint of the consumer, many generalizations emerged, both positive and negative. Overall, one is left with the impression of conscientious, caring teachers trying hard to convey a pre-packaged curriculum to students who are seldom meaningfully engaged. More progress was noted in the curriculum of climate than the curriculum of content. The persistence of traditional methods, procedures, and content, ones usually not developmentally appropriate, was evident. These studies reconfirmed a central truth: *The teacher makes the difference.* It is not the grade organization, interdisciplinary teaming, or anything else that is *the* essential factor in improving middle schools, it is the quality of the classroom teacher.

O'Steen, B., Cuper, P., Spires, H., Beal, C., & Pope, C. (2002). Curriculum integration: Theory, practice, and research for a sustainable future. In V. A. Anfara, Jr. & S. L. Stacki (Eds.), *Middle school curriculum, instruction, and assessment* (pp. 1-21). Greenwich, CT: Information Age Publishing.

O'Steen and several colleagues from North Carolina State University conducted a content analysis across many different research studies on integrated curriculum over the last decade. They focused on units of study that featured, to some degree, "(1) adolescent concerns and input; (2) active inquiry; and (3) action-oriented end products" (p. 11). They discovered that contextual factors (e.g., geography, administrator support, students' backgrounds) strongly influenced the extent to which teachers chose to put into practice these three basic components of integrated curriculum. The researchers assert "the majority of attempts at curriculum integration registered positive reactions" (p. 15). They go on to recommend research, both qualitative and quantitative, to learn more about the influences of context and connections between learning tied to curriculum integration and high-stakes tests.

Pate, P. E., Homestead, E., & McGinnis, K. (1996). *Making integrated curriculum work: Teachers, students, and the quest for a coherent curriculum.* New York: Teachers College Press.

A university professor and two middle school teachers developed this comprehensive description of life on a middle school team where the two teachers and 60 students learned to develop a coherent curriculum together. A coherent curriculum "encompasses meeting the needs of students and teachers, connecting the content, encouraging student voice, and relating schooling to real life, thereby ensuring that student learning is relevant and personally meaningful" (p. xiii). Using observations, interviews, and analysis of artifacts (e.g., student-developed rubrics, teachers' and students' reflective journal entries, student projects), these three teacher-researchers gathered and analyzed data on how teachers and students can together

- Establish a democratic learning environment
- Develop curriculum focused on social and personal issues, tied to standards, and meaningfully connected across subject areas
- Develop and use authentic means of assessing learning.

In addition to representing fine research, *Making Integrated Curriculum Work* also provides a wealth of ideas about how to handle the day-to-day details of planning, teaching, assessing, communicating with parents, sharing governance with middle school students, and gradually moving toward more coherent curriculum over the course of a year.

## Recommended Resources

Brazee, E., & Capelluti, J. (1995). *Dissolving boundaries: Toward an integrative curriculum.* Columbus, OH: National Middle School Association.

Drake, S. M. (1998). *Creating integrated curriculum: Proven ways to increase student learning.* Thousand Oaks, CA: Corwin Press.

Nesin, G., & Lounsbury, J. H. (1999). *Curriculum integration: Twenty questions – with answers.* Atlanta, GA: Georgia Middle School Association.

Siu-Runyan, Y., & Faircloth, V. (Eds.). (1995). *Beyond separate subjects: Integrative learning at the middle level.* Norwood, MA: Christopher-Gordon Publishers.

Springer, M. (1994). *Watershed: A successful voyage into integrative learning.* Columbus, OH: National Middle School Association.

Stevenson, C., & Carr, J. F. (Eds.). (1993). *Integrative studies in the middle grades: Dancing through walls.* New York: Teachers College Press.

Vars, G. F. (1993). *Interdisciplinary teaching: Why and how.* Columbus, OH: National Middle School Association.

## 2. MULTIPLE LEARNING AND TEACHING APPROACHES THAT RESPOND TO THEIR DIVERSITY.

### Research Summary

Each young adolescent is unique, with a particular cultural, experiential, and personal background and a distinctive array of learning styles, interests, talents, and skills. No single teaching method will work for every student; in fact, no single method will work for any one student every day. Instead, research points to the positive impact on student achievement of using varied and appropriate strategies for learning and teaching (Cawelti, 1995; Epstein & Mac Iver, 1992; Russell, 1997).

Given this need for variety in teaching and learning approaches, what does work for students ages 10-15? According to research, young adolescents learn best when students and teachers *together*

- Decide what and how to study, because students learn best when they have some control over their learning (Beane, 1997; Tomlinson, 1999; Wiggins & McTighe, 1998)

- Enhance and accommodate diverse skills, interests, abilities, and talents (Tomlinson, 1999)

- Establish a culturally responsive classroom environment in which students and teachers: understand the diverse cultural backgrounds represented in the classroom; communicate acceptance and positive attitudes about cultural diversity; and build on cultural diversity through day-to-day teaching and learning activities to promote pride, motivation, and improve parents' perceptions of school (Gay, 2000; Shumow & Harris, 1998; Villegas, 1991)

- Build on multiple intelligences (Armstrong, 1994; Gardner, 1983; Gardner & Hatch, 1989)

- Pay attention to learning styles (Dunn & Dunn, 1978; 1987) as student strengths to be built upon and as justification for using a variety of methods (Rosenshine, 1971)

- Connect new learning to prior knowledge and understanding (Bruning, Schraw, & Ronning, 1999)

- Engage in hands-on activities in meaningful contexts (Eggen & Kauchak, 2001; Needels & Knapp, 1994)

- Draw on the community as a resource for learning. Service learning "connects schools and communities in a deliberate effort to construct learning opportunities for youth" (Honig, Kahne, & McLaughlin,

2001, p. 1011). Research shows that service learning can improve student achievement (Melchior, 1997); enhance self-confidence, self-esteem, and self-worth (Conrad & Hedin, 1982; Hamilton & Fezel, 1988); diminish rates of school suspension, school dropout, and school failure (Allen, Philliber, Herrling, & Kuperminc, 1997); decrease alienation and discipline problems among young adolescents (Calabrese & Schumer, 1986).

Teachers should also

- Integrate literacy across the curriculum, using strategies applicable across content areas to enhance learning from texts and using content-specific strategies to improve comprehension (see, for example, Bean, Singer, Sorter, & Frazee, 1986 [World History]; Morrow, Pressley, Smith, & Smith, 1997 [Science]; Siegel & Fonzi, 1995 [Math]).

- Work in collaboration with one another across areas of expertise to adapt teaching and learning approaches given individual student needs. For example, general education teachers can invite special education teachers into the regular classroom to offer suggestions about how best to adapt instruction for students with disabilities (Heward, 1996).

- Communicate and collaborate with families because students benefit from that cooperation, demonstrating higher rates of attendance, improved academic achievement, and an increased willingness to do homework (Cameron & Lee, 1997; Lopez & Scribner, 1999).

Learning and teaching approaches must be varied given the diversity of all types that are represented within any group of middle grades students and the greater likelihood for student success – academic, social, personal, and moral – when those approaches recognize and address students' needs, interests, and talents.

References Cited

Allen, J. P., Philliber, S., Herrling, S., & Kuperminc, G. P. (1997). Preventing teen pregnancy and academic failure: Experimental evaluation of a developmentally based approach. *Child Development, 64*(4), 729-742.

Armstrong, T. (1994). Multiple intelligences: Seven ways to approach curriculum. *Educational Leadership, 52*(3), 26-27.

Bean, T. W., Singer, H., Sorter, J., & Frazee, C. (1986). The effect of metacognitive instruction in outlining and graphic organizer construction on student comprehension in a tenth-grade world history class. *Journal of Reading Behavior, 18,* 153-169.

Beane, J. (1997). *Curriculum integration: Designing the core of democratic education.* New York: Teachers College Press.

Bruning, R., Schraw, G., & Ronning, R. (1999). *Cognitive psychology and instruction* (3rd ed.). Upper Saddle River, NJ: Prentice Hall.

Calabrese, R. L., & Schumer, H. (1986). The effects of service activities on adolescent alienation. *Adolescence, 21,* 675-687.

Cameron, C., & Lee, K. (1997). Bridging the gap between home and school with voice-mail technology. *Journal of Educational Research, 90,* 182-190.

Cawelti, G. (Ed.). (1995). *Handbook of research on improving student achievement.* Arlington, VA: Educational Research Service.

Conrad, D., & Hedin, D. (1982). The impact of experiential education on adolescent development. *Child and Youth Services, 3,* 57-76.

Dunn, R., & Dunn, K. (1978). *Teaching students through their individual learning styles.* Reston, VA: Reston Publishing.

Dunn, R., & Dunn, K. (1987). Dispelling outmoded beliefs about student learning. *Educational Leadership, 44*(6), 55-62.

Eggen, P., & Kauchak, D. (2001). *Educational psychology: Windows on classrooms* (5th ed.). Upper Saddle River, NJ: Prentice Hall.

Epstein, J. L., & Mac Iver, D. J. (1992). *Opportunities to learn: Effects on eighth graders of curriculum offerings and instructional approaches.* Baltimore: Johns Hopkins University Center for Research on Effective Schooling of Disadvantaged Students.

Gardner, H. (1983). *Frames of mind: The theory of multiple intelligences.* New York: Basic Books.

Gardner, H., & Hatch, T. (1989). Multiple intelligences go to school. *Educational Researcher, 18*(8), 4-10.

Gay, G. (2000). *Culturally responsive teaching: Theory, research, and practice.* New York: Teachers College Press.

Hamilton, S. F., & Fenzel, L. M. (1988). The impact of volunteer experience on adolescent social development: Evidence from program effects. *Journal of Adolescent Research, 3*(1), 65-80.

Heward, W. (1996). *Exceptional children* (5th ed.). Upper Saddle River, NJ: Prentice Hall.

Honig, M. I., Kahne, J., & McLaughlin, M. W. (2001). School-community connections: Strengthening opportunity to learn and opportunity to teach. In V. Richardson (Ed.), *Handbook of research on teaching* (4th ed.) (pp. 998-1028). Washington, DC: American Educational Research Association.

Lopez, G., & Scribner, J. (1999, April). *Discourses of involvement: A critical review of parent involvement research.* Paper presented at the annual meeting of the American Educational Research Association, Montreal.

Melchior, A. (1997). *National evaluation of Learn and Serve America school and community-based programs.* Waltham, MA: Center for Human Resources, Brandeis University.

Morrow, L. M., Pressley, M., Smith, J. K., & Smith, M. (1997). The effect of a literature-based program integrated into literacy and science instruction with children from diverse backgrounds. *Reading Research Quarterly, 32,* 55-76.

Needels, M., & Knapp, M. (1994). Teaching writing to children who are underserved. *Journal of Educational Psychology, 86*(3), 339-349.

Rosenshine, B. (1971). *Teaching behaviors and student achievement.* London: National Foundation for Educational Research.

Russell, J. F. (1997). Relationships between the implementation of middle-level program concepts and student achievement. *Journal of Curriculum and Supervision, 12,* 152-168.

Shumow, L., & Harris, W. (1998, April). *Teachers' thinking about home-school relations in low-income urban communities.* Paper presented at the annual meeting of the American Educational Research Association, San Diego, CA.

Siegel, M., & Fonzi, J. M. (1995). The practice of reading in an inquiry-oriented mathematics class. *Reading Research Quarterly, 30,* 632-673.

Tomlinson, C. A. (1999). *The differentiated classroom: Responding to the needs of all learners.* Alexandria, VA: Association for Supervision and Curriculum Development.

Villegas, A. (1991). *Culturally responsive pedagogy for the 1990s and beyond.* Princeton, NJ: Educational Testing Service.

Wiggins, G., & McTighe, J. (1998). *Understanding by design.* Alexandria, VA: Association for Supervision and Curriculum Development

## Annotated References

Daniels, H., & Bizar, M. (1998). *Methods that matter: Six structures for best practice classrooms.* Portland, ME: Stenhouse.

The authors suggest that six basic structures constitute "best practice" in classrooms:

- Integrative units
- Small group activities
- Representing-to-learn
- Classroom workshop
- Authentic experiences
- Reflective assessment.

If teachers use these six structures to characterize the teaching and learning in their classrooms, they will be operating in the long tradition of progressive education and in line with the more recent recommendations of national groups regarding the nature of content knowledge and skills (e.g,. National Council of Teachers of Mathematics, National Science Teachers Association, the Center for the Study of Reading). Grounding their arguments in the research literature and in more than a decade of experience in the Chicago Public Schools, Daniels and Bizar describe each of the six structures in detail, offering classroom examples and explicitly describing the connections between theories and their definition of best practice.

Eyler, J., & Giles, D. E., Jr. (1999). *Where's the learning in service learning?* San Francisco: Jossey-Bass.

The authors draw on two national research projects in documenting the impact service learning has on students' learning. Comparing Models of Service Learning combined a large national survey on attitudes and perceptions of learning with intensive student interviews before and after a service learning experience. The second research project focused on the process of service learning, highlighting reflection in particular, and included interviews with 67 students across seven colleges and universities. In summarizing their findings, Eyler and Giles say, "Service learning makes a difference, and within the group who experience these programs, higher-quality service learning makes a bigger difference" (p. xvii). This book outlines the findings regarding outcomes related to service learning (e.g., understanding and application, critical thinking, personal and interpersonal) and the process of service learning, including what makes a service learning program or experience effective.

Tomlinson, C. A. (1999). *The differentiated classroom: Responding to the needs of all learners.* Alexandria, VA: Association for Supervision and Curriculum Development.

Tomlinson's oft-cited work on differentiating instruction for students of varying needs, abilities, and interests is a vital resource for those who seek to adapt teaching to students, instead of trying to adapt students to teaching. Tomlinson drew on her work with teachers and in classrooms across the country to develop her description of a differentiated classroom's key elements:

- The teacher focuses on the essentials (concepts, principles, and skills)
- The teacher attends to student differences (experiences, culture, gender, prior knowledge)
- Assessment and instruction are inseparable (assessment is diagnostic)
- The teacher modifies content, process, and products given students' varying points of readiness, interests, and learning profiles
- All students participate in respectful work, e.g., all students are expected to grow and to have support for their continued growth
- The teacher and students collaborate in learning
- The teacher balances group and individual norms, helping each student be the best he or she can possibly be
- The teacher and student work together flexibly, using materials, space, grouping strategies, and instructional strategies in differing ways. (pp. 9-14)

Tomlinson describes differentiated learning classrooms in detail, offering examples, strategies, and recommendations for moving toward differentiation and away from traditional, teacher-centered approaches.

Wiggins, G., & McTighe, J. (1998). *Understanding by design.* Alexandria, VA: Association for Supervision and Curriculum Development.

Wiggins and McTighe build on their extensive experience with classroom assessment to develop an "education for understanding" (p. 3) supported by backward design. The backward design process includes three stages:

(1) Identify desired results: What should students know, understand, and be able to do?

(2) Determine acceptable evidence: How will we know if students have achieved the desired results?

(3) Plan learning experiences and instruction: What enabling knowledge and skills will students need to perform effectively? What activities will equip students with the needed knowledge and skills? What materials and resources are best suited to accomplish these goals? (pp. 9-13)

The book includes examples, design templates, descriptions of methods for helping students achieve understanding, and addresses the role of students' misunderstandings in making decisions about teaching.

## Recommended Resources

Fertman, C. I., White, G. P., & White, L. J. (1996). *Service learning in the middle school: Building a culture of service.* Columbus, OH: National Middle School Association.

Harmin, M. (1994). *Inspiring active learning: A handbook for teachers.* Alexandria, VA: Association for Supervision and Curriculum Development.

Lewis, B. A. (1995). *The kid's guide to service projects: Over 500 service ideas for young people who want to make a difference.* Minneapolis, MN: Free Spirit Publishing.

Sadler, C. R. (2001). *Comprehension strategies for middle grades learners: A handbook for content area teachers.* Newark, DE: International Reading Association.

Schurr, S. (1995). *Prescriptions for success in heterogeneous classrooms.* Columbus, OH: National Middle School Association.

Wood, K. D., & Harmon, J. M. (2001). *Strategies for integrating reading and writing in middle and high school classrooms.* Westerville, OH: National Middle School Association.

3. ASSESSMENT AND EVALUATION PROGRAMS THAT PROMOTE QUALITY LEARNING.

## Research Summary

In the last 40 years, layer upon layer of tests have been added so that we now have district-wide, state-wide, national, and international assessment programs operating simultaneously (Stiggins, 2002). On January 8, 2002, President Bush signed school reform legislation that required even more standardized tests of every student in mathematics and reading every year in grades three through eight (*No Child Left Behind Act of 2001*). Even with this push for high-stakes testing, middle grades educators and experts in the field of assessment advocate for assessment and evaluation that will promote student learning – assessment that is an integral and dynamic part of curriculum and instruction (e.g., Jackson & Davis, 2000; National Forum to Accelerate Middle-Grades Reform, 2002; National Middle School Association, 1995; Shepard, 2000; Stiggins, 2002; Thompson, 2002) – not with the idea of avoiding reform and accountability, but with the conviction that assessment should "lead to high expectations, foster high-quality instruction, and support higher levels of learning for every student" (National Forum to Accelerate Middle-Grades Reform, http://www.mgforum.org).

In order to support higher levels of learning for each student, research indicates that it is important to include a variety of assessments that go beyond traditional paper and pencil tests but do not necessarily exclude traditional forms of assessment (Leon & Elias, 1998). Portfolios and performance assessments are two types of alternative assessment that teachers, students, and parents have struggled with but were found beneficial for students' learning and motivation (e.g. Baron, Johnson, & Acor, 1998; Lockledge & Hayn, 2000; Leon, & Elias, 1998; Saurino & Saurino, 1996; Thompson, 2002). Other assessment strategies include journals, projects, presentations, and simulations (Pate, Homestead, & McGinnis, 1997); students' self-assessment of their own work (The President and Fellows of Harvard College, 2000; Shepard, 2000; Wolf, Bixby, Glenn, & Gardner, 1991); as well as student-led conferences (Kinney, Munroe, & Sessions, 2000).

Current research also points to the critical role of formative assessment in young adolescents' learning and the way to include it appropriately in the classroom (Black & Wiliam, 1998). That is, given certain conditions, formative assessment makes a significant difference in student achievement, particularly for low-achieving students. For example, giving frequent short tests rather than infrequent longer tests is a good strategy for checking certain levels of knowledge but may be ineffective for improving students' learning if students do not receive substantive feedback that is personal and relevant to their mistakes. If formative assessment is to function effectively in a middle grades classroom, it is also important that students be actively engaged in learning, teachers systematically use the results of the formative assessment to make adjustments in their teaching, students learn to self-assess so that they will understand the main purpose of their learning, and teachers give feedback that tells students how they can improve and do not make comparisons between students.

For such changes to occur in the way middle school teachers view assessment, a change in the overall culture of the school may be necessary so that new methods of assessment become a part of teachers' belief systems, rather than merely a new innovation (Thompson, 2002). If so, some of the structures that must be in place include: (1) the school and its teachers must come to view themselves as a learning community; (2) there must be proactive leadership at the district and building level; (3) teachers must have access to ongoing, meaningful, and relevant professional development; (4) teachers must have time for collaboration; (5) teachers need an opportunity to understand new research in the cognitive sciences; and (6) coherent and congruent curriculum, instruction, and assessment must be in place or must be developed.

In summary, as middle grades educators seek to balance what at times seems like an overwhelming emphasis on standardized testing with classroom assessment and evaluation that is designed to promote quality learning, they need to understand that effective assessment for young adolescents involves more than adopting a few new assessment strategies. It involves rethinking the way curriculum, instruction, and assessment relate to each other and to student learning. It takes work, time, and effort but results in students who are more interested in and more engaged in learning.

## References Cited

Baron, R. W., Johnson, C. J., & Acor, S. (1998). Portfolio assessments: Involving students in their journey to success. *Schools in the Middle, 7*(3), 32-35.

Black, P., & Wiliam, D. (1998). Inside the black box: Raising standards through classroom assessment. *Phi Delta Kappan, 80*(2), 139-145.

Jackson, A. W., & Davis, G. A. (2000). *Turning points 2000: Educating adolescents in the 21st century.* New York: Teachers College Press.

Kinney, P., Munroe, M. B., & Sessions, P. (2000). *A school-wide approach to student-led conferences: A practitioner's guide.* Westerville, OH: National Middle School Association.

Leon, S., & Elias, M. (1998). A comparison of portfolio, performance, and traditional assessment in the middle school. *Research in Middle Level Education Quarterly, 21*(2), 21-37.

Lockledge, A., & Hayn, J. (Eds.). (2000). *Using portfolios across the curriculum.* Westerville, OH: National Middle School Association.

National Forum to Accelerate Middle-Grades Reform. (2002). *High-stakes testing.* Newton, MA: Author. Retrieved July 24, 2003, from http://www.mgforum.org/policy.asp

National Middle School Association. (1995). *This we believe: Developmentally responsive middle level schools.* Columbus, OH: Author.

*No Child Left Behind Act of 2001.* Public Law 107-110, 107th Cong., Cong. Rec. 1425. (2001). (enacted 2002).

Pate, P. E., Homestead, E. R., & McGinnis, K. L. (1997). *Making integrated curriculum work: Teachers, students, and the quest for coherent curriculum.* New York: Teachers College Press.

The President and Fellows of Harvard College. (2000). *Rubrics and self assessment project.* Cambridge, MA: Harvard Graduate School of Education. Retrieved July 24, 2003, from http://www.pz/Harvard.edu/Research/RubricSelf.htm

Saurino, D. R., & Saurino, P. L. (1996). Collaborative teacher research: An investigation of alternative assessment. *Current Issues in Middle Level Education, 5*(2), 50-72.

Shepard, L. A. (2000). The role of assessment in a learning culture. *Educational Researcher, 29*(7), 4-14.

Stiggins, R. J. (2002). Assessment crisis: The absence of assessment *FOR* learning. *Phi Delta Kappan, 83*(10), 758-765.

Thompson, S. (2002). Reculturing middle schools to use cross-curricular portfolios to support integrated learning. In V. A. Anfara, Jr. & S. L. Stacki (Eds.), *Middle school curriculum, instruction, and assessment* (pp. 157-179). Greenwich, CT: Information Age Publishing.

Wolf, D., Bixby, J., Glenn, J., & Gardner, H. (1991). To use their minds well: Investigating new forms of student assessment. *Review of Research in Education, 17,* 31-74.

## Annotated References

Baron, R. W., Johnson, C. J., & Acor, S. (1998). Portfolio assessments: Involving students in their journey to success. *Schools in the Middle, 7*(3), 32-35.

This year-long, site-based evaluation examines the implementation of portfolio assessment combined with the use of behavioral descriptors called Performance Results to guide instruction for middle level students in one middle school in Utah's Salt Lake City School District. From their experiences, Baron, Johnson, and Acor found that there were stumbling blocks for teachers and students including students' and teachers' initial difficulty connecting standards to particular assignments, students' difficulty with self-assessment, storage, and lost artifacts as portfolios were carried from class to class or home at the end of the grading period. They also found positive outcomes – teachers improved in their ability to incorporate the performance results in their curricula which shifted the focus to students as lifelong learners, students developed a sense of pride in their portfolios and the work they had done and improved in their reflections and self-assessment, and parents were more engaged in their student's work and felt more informed about assignments.

Black, P., & Wiliam, D. (1998). Inside the black box: Raising standards through classroom assessment. *Phi Delta Kappan, 80*(2), 139-145.

Through an extensive review of research (9 years of 160 journals and earlier reviews of research) that yielded 580 articles and chapters, 250 of which were chosen, the authors examined the importance of formative assessment in classroom work. Specifically, they found that there is evidence that improving formative assessment results in significant gains in achievement (effect size 0.4-0.7) across age groups, content areas, and countries. Furthermore, in many studies, improved formative assessment helped low achievers more than other students, thus narrowing the gap in student achievement while raising overall achievement. At the same time, the research shows that there is need for improvement in formative assessment and there is evidence that shows ways to make the needed improvements. In particular, research shows that teachers need to provide students more substantive, more specific feedback on assessments; teachers also need to view students' self-assessment as a critical component of formative assessment.

Leon, S., & Elias, M. (1998). A comparison of portfolio, performance, and traditional assessment in the middle school. *Research in Middle Level Education Quarterly, 21*(2), 21-37.

The purpose of this single-site study was to examine the way sixth grade students enrolled in an Organizational Study Skills course performed when assessed with portfolio and performance tasks and to compare their performance on these authentic methods of assessment to their performance on more traditional measures of assessment (e.g., report card grades and standardized test scores). Students were randomly assigned to two different groups and, at the end of the course, were asked, depending on their group, either to compile a portfolio of their work or to complete a project to demonstrate the skills they learned in the class. Using descriptive statistical analysis, the researchers reported that 40 percent of the students scored higher on the two authentic measures of assessment than they did on the more traditional measures and another 26 percent scored equally well on both types thus providing support for middle school teachers using a variety of assessment strategies, including traditional paper and pencil tests, portfolios, and performance tasks, in order to give all students adequate opportunities to demonstrate their abilities.

The President and Fellows of Harvard College. (2000). *Rubrics and self-assessment project.* Cambridge, MA: Harvard Graduate School of Education. Retrieved July 24, 2003, from http://www.pz.harvard.edu/Research/RubricSelf.htm

Two short-term studies, involving seventh and eighth graders in two urban middle schools, examined the effect of rubrics on students' writing. In the first study, eighth graders were asked to write three different essays (persuasive, autobiographical incident, and historical fiction). Students in the treatment classes were given an instructional rubric before writing each essay, while students in the control classes were not – they were simply told to write first and second drafts of their essay. The results show that the treatment group scored significantly higher on one of the three essays than the control group; and students in the treatment group, when surveyed, had a much clearer understanding of the criteria for good writing. For study two, students in 13 seventh and eighth grade classes in the same two urban schools were asked to write essays with all students receiving the instructional rubric. The treatment classes engaged in a guided self-assessment process where students were to examine their writing in class using the criteria outlined on the instructional rubric. The results of the second study suggest that the self-assessment process may have a positive effect on girls' writing, but no effect on boys' writing. Together these studies indicate that rubrics, used with careful instructions in the classroom, may have a positive effect on students' writing.

Thompson, S. (2002). Reculturing middle schools to use cross-curricular portfolios to support integrated learning. In V. A. Anfara, Jr. & S. L. Stacki (Eds.), *Middle school curriculum, instruction, and assessment* (pp. 157-179). Greenwich, CT: Information Age Publishing.

This five-year, multi-site case study of five middle schools in a single mid-western district was designed to investigate the conditions needed to "reculture" schools for young adolescents so that they would support the institutionalization of curriculum integration and cross-curricular portfolios. The participants included 120 teachers and 10 administrators – one principal, and one assistant principal from each of the five schools. Data were collected through interviews and informal conversations with individuals and groups, observations, and a review of formal and informal documents, allowing for triangulation of data. From her study, Thompson concluded there are six conditions necessary to sustain change in something as complex as practices related to student learning, such as integrated curriculum and cross-curricular portfolios in middle schools.

## Recommended Resources

Herman, J. L., Aschbacher, P. R., & Winters, L. (1992). *A practical guide to alternative assessment.* Alexandria, VA: Association for Supervision and Curriculum Development.

Lockledge, A., & Hayn, J. (Eds.). (2000). *Using portfolios across the curriculum.* Westerville, OH: National Middle School Association.

Lounsbury, J., & Schurr, S. (2003). *Assessing student progress: Moving from grades to portfolios* (Professional Development Kit #4). Westerville, OH: National Middle School Association.

Lustig, K. (1996). *Portfolio assessment: A handbook for middle level teachers.* Columbus, OH: National Middle School Association.

National Middle School Association. (2002). *NMSA research summary #16: What are appropriate assessment practices for middle school students?* Retrieved July 24, 2003, from http://nmsa.org/

Stowell, L. P., & McDaniel, J. E. (1997). The changing face of assessment. In J. L. Irvin (Ed.), *What current research says to the middle level practitioner* (pp. 137-150). Columbus, OH: National Middle School Association.

Vars, G. (2001). Assessment and learning that promote learning. In T. O. Erb (Ed.), *This we believe . . . And now we must act* (pp. 78-89). Westerville, OH: National Middle School Association.

Wiggins, G. (1998). *Educative assessment: Designing assessments to inform and improve performance.* San Francisco: Jossey-Bass.

Wiggins, G., & McTighe, J. (1998). *Understanding by design.* Alexandria, VA: Association for Supervision and Curriculum Development.

## 4. ORGANIZATIONAL STRUCTURES THAT SUPPORT MEANINGFUL RELATIONSHIPS AND LEARNING.

### Research Summary

Over the past decade the research literature on middle level organizational structures has increased considerably. The majority of this research focuses on implementing interdisciplinary teaming and its effect on schools, teachers, and student learning and achievement (Arhar, 1990; Arhar, Johnston, & Markle, 1989; Dickinson & Erb, 1997; Flowers, Mertens, & Mulhall, 2000). Several studies have focused on the number of schools that are implementing teaming, common planning time, and other middle level organizational structures (McEwin, Dickinson, & Jenkins, 2003; Valentine, Clark, Hackman, & Petzko, 2002; Warren & Muth, 1995). Additionally, these studies report on the occurrence of varying student grouping strategies and scheduling arrangements contained in schools across the country (George & Alexander, 2003; George & Lounsbury, 2000). A 1993 study found that 87 percent of principals in exemplary schools indicated that interdisciplinary teaming was moderately or well developed at their schools (George & Shewey, 1994). A national longitudinal study reports that the incidence of interdisciplinary teaming has increased since 1988 (McEwin, Dickinson, & Jenkins, 2003). In 2001, 77 percent of principals reported the use of teaming as compared to 52 percent in 1993 and 30 percent in 1988. Another recent study conducted in 2000 found that 79 percent of middle level principals report that their schools had one or more interdisciplinary teams (Valentine, Clark, Hackman, & Petzko, 2002). A similar study conducted in 1992 by the same researchers found that only 52 percent of principals reported the implementation of teaming. Since the mid-1980s, there has been an increase in the number of middle level schools that have embraced the concept of interdisciplinary teaming. As many practitioners and researchers are quite aware, simply creating the team structures within a middle level school is not enough – effective teaming requires much more.

While the implementation of teaming is important, the effectiveness of teaming is dependent on factors such as the frequency and amount of common planning time, number of students per team, the length of time or experience in teaming, and professional development focused on effective teaming practices. Current research has begun to address these factors and the interrelationships that exist among them, however, more research is needed. We are beginning to better understand the complex relationships that exist between team size, teaming experience, and the role of professional development in teaming practices.

Overall, the effects of student grouping, sub-dividing schools into smaller learning environments (e.g., houses), and the impact of the physical school structure (e.g., age, layout, size) have not been well studied. Likewise, research on scheduling, looping, staffing, and teachers making flexible use of time, space, staff, and grouping arrangements tends to focus more on what is currently being implemented and to a lesser degree on the effect of implementation on student learning. Numerous qualitative studies exist that focus on studying these traits or characteristics at one or a small sample of schools and/or classrooms. However, it is difficult to generalize the results of such studies to larger groups of schools or schools with different characteristics (e.g., school location, student socioeconomic status, student ethnicity).

While the current research base for middle level organizational structures is promising, there is still a critical need for additional research specifically focused on how these structures impact student learning and achievement. More large-scale quantitative studies that demonstrate reliability and provide generalizability across many schools and more rigorous studies that employ not only qualitative and quantitative methodologies but also meta-analyses of the various middle level components and how they interrelate are needed. Finally, in order for middle level research to impact teaching and learning and the policies that influence them, the research must be made accessible to those who truly need it – teachers, administrators, and policymakers.

## References Cited

Arhar, J. (1990). Interdisciplinary teaming as a school intervention to increase the social bonding of middle level students. *Research in Middle Level Education: Selected Studies 1990.* Columbus, OH: National Middle School Association.

Arhar, J., Johnston, J. H., & Markle, G. C. (1989). The effects of teaming on students. *Middle School Journal, 20*(3), 21-27.

Dickinson, T. S., & Erb, T. O. (1997). *We gain more than we give: Teaming in middle schools.* Columbus, OH: National Middle School Association.

Flowers, N., Mertens, S., & Mulhall, P. (2000). What makes interdisciplinary teams effective? *Middle School Journal, 31*(4), 53-56.

George, P. S., & Alexander, W. M. (2003). *The exemplary middle school* (3rd ed.). Belmont, CA: Thomson/Wadsworth Learning.

George, P. S., & Lounsbury, J. H. (2000). *Making big schools feel small: Multiage grouping, looping, and schools-within-a-school.* Westerville, OH: National Middle School Association.

George, P. S., & Shewey, K. (1994). *New evidence for the middle school.* Columbus, OH: National Middle School Association.

McEwin, C. K., Dickinson, T. S., & Jenkins, D. M. (2003). *America's middle schools in the new century: Status and progress.* Westerville, OH: National Middle School Association.

Valentine, J. W., Clark, D. C., Hackman, D. G., & Petzko, V. N. (2002). *A national study of leadership in middle level schools. Volume 1: A national study of middle level leaders and school programs.* Reston, VA: National Association of Secondary School Principals.

Warren, L. L., & Muth, K. D. (1995). The impact of common planning time on middle grade students and teachers. *Research in Middle level Education, 18(3),* 41-58.

## Annotated References

Brown, D. F. (2001). Middle level teachers' perceptions of the impact of block scheduling on instruction and learning. *Research in Middle Level Education Annual, 24,* 121-141.

This qualitative study focuses on the implementation of a 4 x 4 block schedule and its perceived effects on instructional strategies and curricular decision making. Ten teachers from two middle level schools (one 6-8 suburban school and one 7-8 rural school) were interviewed to ascertain the effect of the block schedule. Respondents report the use of more active instructional strategies. The majority of respondents believe that the amount of curricula studied must be altered to adjust to this alternative scheduling format. Teachers believe block scheduling positively influenced student learning. The 4 x 4 semester block schedule was not found to promote the development of interdisciplinary studies or teacher teaming.

Felner, R. D., Jackson, A. W., Kasak, D., Mulhall, P., Brand, S. & Flowers, N. (1997). The impact of school reform for the middle years: Longitudinal study of a network engaged in Turning Points-based comprehensive school transformation. *Phi Delta Kappan, 78*(7), 528-532, 541-550.

This study addresses the impact of Turning Points recommendations on 31 middle level schools participating in the Illinois Middle Grades Network in 1991-92. Schools were classified into one of three levels of implementation based on the level of structural changes (e.g., implementation of teaming, frequency of common planning time, lower numbers of students per team, frequency of advisory periods). More highly implemented schools were found to have higher levels of student achievement and student self-esteem, combined with lower levels of student reports of worry and fear. The study cautions about the need to view the *Turning Points* recommendations as interrelated and not simply as a list of elements to be checked off as they are "implemented." The authors feel that the implementation of these elements is necessary but not sufficient to become an exemplary middle level school.

Flowers, N., Mertens, S., & Mulhall, P. (1999). The impact of teaming: Five research-based outcomes of teaming. *Middle School Journal, 31*(2), 57-60.

This article describes and discusses five research-based outcomes of interdisciplinary teaming. The analyses are based on a sample of 155 middle level schools in Michigan. Quantitative data were collected through a self-study assessment consisting of written surveys completed by teachers, students, and principals. Qualitative data were collected through telephone interviews with the schools. The study yielded five outcomes of interdisciplinary teaming: (1) common planning is a critical component, (2) teaming improves school work climate, (3) teaming increases parent contact, (4) teaming increases job satisfaction, and (5) teaming has a positive effect on student achievement.

George, P. S., & Lounsbury, J. H. (2000). *Making big schools feel small: Multiage grouping, looping, and schools-within-a-school.* Westerville, OH: National Middle School Association.

This book describes ways of creating small communities for learning within increasingly larger schools and enhancing long-term teacher-student relationships. The first two chapters review the relevant literature and discuss why smallness and long-term teacher-student relationships are important for young adolescents. The authors then examine three ways in which such relationships can be achieved: (1) multiage grouping, (2) looping, and (3) schools-within-a-school. Research on middle school organizational patterns is also summarized. The last part of the book presents the findings of a national survey on long-term teacher-student relationships that gathered the opinions of 105 educators, 586 parents, and 1,100 students from 33 schools. Overall, teachers practicing long-term teacher-student relationships perceived substantial benefits (e.g., classroom management, accurate diagnosis of student needs, development of a sense of community among students and teachers). Students and parents reported similar attitudes concerning the benefits of long-term teacher-student relationships. The book concludes with a set of guidelines for practitioners interested in implementing long-term teacher-student relationships to make big schools seem small.

George, P. S., & Shewey, K. (1994). *New evidence for the middle school.* Columbus, OH: National Middle School Association.

The results presented here were derived from two large-scale studies: one conducted in 1985 and a follow-up study in 1993. Middle school administrators across the country were asked to respond to written surveys focused on the implementation of the middle school concept (e.g., teaming, flexible scheduling, advisory, school climate) in their schools. In the 1985 study, 130 out of 160 schools (81%) participated; the 1993 study included 108 out of 300 schools (36%). Many of the participating schools had been previously identified as exemplary, indicating a higher level of implementation of at least some middle school concepts. The 1993 survey yielded the following findings: (1) the majority of schools reported implementing most of the middle school programmatic components; (2) the interdisciplinary organization of teachers was central to schools that have implemented the middle school concept for many years; (3) advisor-advisee programs, school buildings specifically designed to be middle schools, and foreign language programs, among others, were not found to be critical components in the long-term effectiveness of middle schools; and (4) when effectively implemented, the middle school concept leads to positive outcomes, including improved academic achievement and attendance, lower rates of disciplinary problems, and improved relationships between and among students, teachers, and parents.

Lee, V., & Smith, J. (1993). Effects of school restructuring on the achievement and engagement of middle-grades students. *Sociology of Education, 66*(3), 164-187.

Lee and Smith conducted a multivariate study of middle grade students to examine the impact of attending "restructured schools" on student achievement and engagement. A sample of nearly 9,000 eighth-grade students in 377 schools was drawn from the 1988 National Education Longitudinal Study (NELS) to assess the impact of reduced departmental structures, heterogeneous grouping practices, and team teaching on student outcomes, including student achievement, engagement in academic work, and at-risk behaviors (e.g., disciplinary problems). Modest but consistent positive effects of restructuring were found on both student achievement and engagement.

## Recommended Resources

Arnold, J., & Stevenson, C. (1998). *Teachers' teaming handbook: A middle level planning guide.* Fort Worth, TX: Harcourt Brace.

*Block scheduling: Research and resources.* (2002). Retrieved April 30, 2003, from the University of Minnesota, College of Education and Human Development, Center for Applied Research and Educational Improvement: http://www.education.umn.edu/ CAREI/Blockscheduling/Resources/default.html

Hackman, D. G., & Valentine, J. W. (1998). Designing an effective middle level schedule. *Middle School Journal, 29*(5), 3-13.

Kain, D. L. (1998). *Camel makers: Building effective teacher teams together.* Columbus, OH: National Middle School Association.

Rottier, J. (2001). *Implementing and improving teaming: A handbook for middle level leaders.* Westerville, OH: National Middle School Association.

Rottier, J. (2002). *Taking teaming to the next level: The principal's role.* Westerville, OH: National Middle School Association.

Schurr, S., & Lounsbury, J. (2001). *Revitalizing teaming to improve student learning* (Professional Development Kit #3). Westerville, OH: National Middle School Association.

Williamson, R. (1993). *Scheduling the middle level school.* Reston, VA: National Association of Secondary School Principals.

## 5. SCHOOL-WIDE EFFORTS AND POLICIES THAT FOSTER HEALTH, WELLNESS, AND SAFETY.

### Research Summary

The importance of providing a safe, healthy, and supportive learning environment for young adolescents has been recognized and promoted for decades. It serves as a central tenet or core principle of nearly all middle school reform recommendations and models. Numerous studies have focused on varying aspects of safe and supportive learning environments, including: comprehensive health and fitness programs, development and inclusion of health curricula, collaborations with local health and social support agencies, school safety, violence prevention, risk behaviors (e.g., alcohol, tobacco, drugs), latchkey status, and a sense of social adjustment and school community (e.g., dropout, climate, sense of belonging) (Call, Reidel, Hein, McLoyd, Peterson, & Kipke, 2002; Dryfoos, 1994; Finn, 1989; Hamburg, 1997; Hechinger, 1992; Schultz, 2001). Each of these areas is critically important to the welfare, adjustment, and achievement of middle level students.

The research literature provides overwhelming evidence that the middle level years are "the last best chance" to affect these students' futures. It is during the middle school years that young adolescents begin experimenting with a range of risky behaviors such as alcohol, tobacco, drug use, and unprotected sex. Based on several large-scale studies, Dryfoos (1998) concluded that 10 percent of 14-year-olds in 1995 were at "very high risk" based on their involvement in high-risk behaviors. Resnick and associates (1997) found that parent-family connectedness and perceived school connectedness were protective against every health risk behavior measure except history of pregnancy. Conversely, ease of access to guns at home was associated with suicide and violence. Access to substances in the home was associated with cigarettes, alcohol, and marijuana use among all students. Appearing "older than most" in class was associated with substance use and an earlier age of sexual debut among both junior and senior high students. Repeating a grade in school was associated with emotional distress among students in junior high and high school and with tobacco use among junior high students. On the other hand, parental expectations regarding school achievement were associated with lower levels of health risk behaviors; parental disapproval of early sexual debut was associated with a later age of onset of intercourse.

Obviously, many middle level schools could benefit from comprehensive school health programs (CSHP). Such programs seek to reduce or eliminate health-related barriers to student academic and personal success (National Middle School Association, 2003). CSHP are designed to reinforce health-promoting behaviors in students and to provide the skills students need to avoid negative health practices. Some of the components of a CSHP include health education, health services, physical education, counseling and social services, and the integration of community resources. These components provide additional opportunities, supports, and services that many of today's students need to be successful (MacLaury, 2000; Reyes & Fowler, 1999). Although the components listed above are present in many schools, few schools have developed a comprehensive, seamless web of care frequently termed a "full-service" school (Dryfoos, 1994). "Full-service" schools develop multi-faceted comprehensive programs that build knowledge, attitudes, and skills that promote health and reinforce the behaviors that prevent future problems.

The research literature focuses primarily on individual components of student well-being. There are numerous studies specific to student safety, violence prevention, health curricula, physical education programs, approaches to peer-mediation, and the outcomes of high-risk behavior (e.g., alcohol, tobacco, and drug use). Currently there are very few large-scale studies that have examined young adolescent health and safety issues from a comprehensive perspective. Such studies, while potentially time intensive and costly, provide results that are more likely to influence and promote policy decisions concerning "best practices" for students in middle level schools.

## References Cited

Call, K. T., Riedel, A. A., Hein, K., McLoyd, V., Peterson, A., & Kipke, M. (2002). Adolescent health and well-being in the twenty-first century: A global perspective. *Journal of Research on Adolescence, 12*(1), 69-98.

Dryfoos, J. G. (1994). *Full-service schools: A revolution in health and social services for children, youth, and families.* San Francisco: Jossey-Bass.

Dryfoos, J. (1998). *Safe passage: Making it through adolescence in a risky society.* New York: Oxford University Press.

Finn, J. D. (1989). Withdrawing from school. *Review of Educational Research, 59* (2), 117-142.

Hamburg, B. (1997). Education for healthy futures: Health promotion and life skills training. In R. Takanishi & D. A. Hamburg (Eds.), *Preparing adolescents for the twenty-first century: Challenges facing Europe and the United States* (pp. 108-135). New York: Cambridge University Press.

Hechinger, R. M. (1992). *Fateful choices: Healthy youth for the 21st century.* New York: Carnegie Council on Adolescent Development.

MacLaury, S. (2000). Teaching prevention by infusing health education into advisory programs. *Middle School Journal, 31*(5), 51-56.

National Middle School Association. (2003). *NMSA Research Summary #13: Comprehensive school health programs.* Retrieved July 24, 2003 from http://www.nmsa.org

Resnick, M. D., Bearman, P. S., Blum, R. W., Bauman, K. E., Harris, K. M., Jones, J., et al. (1997). Protecting adolescents from harm. Findings from the National Longitudinal Study on Adolescent Health. *Journal of the American Medical Association, 278,* 823-832.

Reyes, A., & Fowler, M. (1999). Healthy minds in healthy bodies: Adolescent clinics and middle schools in collaboration. *Middle School Journal, 30*(5), 7-12.

Schultz, J. (2001). Programs and policies that foster health, wellness, and safety. In T. O. Erb, (Ed.), *This we believe...And now we must act* (pp. 99-107). Westerville, OH: National Middle School Association.

## Annotated References

Lockwood, D. (1997). *Violence among middle school and high school students: Analysis and implications for prevention.* Washington, DC: Department of Justice.

The type and frequency of violent incidents are identified, but the focus is on factors such as the relationship among the antagonists, the sequence of events and escalations, and the goals and justifications cited by students. Information is drawn from in-depth interviews with 110 students from public schools with high levels of violence. The 110 students, 86 of whom were African Americans, reported 250 incidents of violence. Data show that the problem of violence is growing, as is juveniles' risk of victimization. The design of this study was chosen to provide information that can be used in the curricula of school-based conflict resolution programs. In the largest proportion of incidents, the first step was relatively minor, but escalated. About five percent eventually involved a gun. Most incidents took place among young people who knew each other, and most incidents started in the school or the home. The most common goal was retribution, followed by an attempt to bring about compliance, self-defense, or defense of one's image. Justifications offered for the incidents stemmed from a value system in which violence was acceptable. In using the findings in violence prevention programs, reducing the frequency of opening moves may be the most promising approach.

Mertens, S. B., Flowers, N., & Mulhall, P. F. (2003). Should middle grades students be left alone after school? *Middle School Journal, 34*(5), 57-61.

This study on latchkey students is based on a sample of over 121,000 students attending 287 middle grades schools in Arkansas, Louisiana, Michigan, and Mississippi during 2000-01. The demographics of the student sample are quite diverse with schools located in urban, suburban, and rural areas. Nearly 50 percent of students reported receiving a free/reduced lunch and 40 percent identified themselves as an ethnic minority. Based on survey responses, students were classified into one of three latchkey categories: (1) no days home alone after school, (2) less than three hours home alone, and (3) three or more hours home alone. The most significant finding was that when students are left home alone for three hours or more after school (regardless of the number of days), their reports of self-esteem and academic efficacy are much lower and their levels of depression and behavior problems are much higher. Interestingly, students home alone for less than three hours had comparable outcomes to those who report not being home alone after school.

National Center for Education Statistics. (2000). *In the middle: Characteristics of public schools with a focus on middle schools* (NCES 2000-312). Jessup, MD: U. S. Department of Education.

    This report uses data from the Schools and Staffing Survey (SASS), a nationally representative survey conducted in 1987-88, 1990-91, and 1993-94 to describe various aspects of middle level schools, examine how they have changed over time, and compare middle level schools to elementary and secondary schools. The report focuses primarily on the 1993-94 SASS that contains data from teachers and principals in over 82,000 schools across the country. One area examined was health-related services. General medical care was provided by 60 percent of all schools and diagnostic services by 82 percent; at least 90 percent of schools had drug and alcohol prevention programs. The proportion of schools providing substance abuse counseling increased from elementary to middle level to high school. At least 50 percent of middle level and secondary schools provided this service in 1993-94, compared to 26 percent for elementary schools.

North Carolina State Department of Public Instruction. (1996). *Middle school risk behavior 1995 survey results.* Raleigh, NC: Division of Accountability Services.

    This study reports the results of the 1995 Youth Risk Behavior Survey (YRBS) Middle School Questionnaire. The survey measured health risk behaviors, including: (1) weapons and violence; (2) suicide-related behaviors; (3) vehicle safety; (4) tobacco, alcohol, and other drug use; and (5) nutrition and physical exercise. A total of 2,227 students from 53 North Carolina public schools were surveyed. Results within the personal safety category showed that weapon use is predominantly a male activity, with 20 percent carrying weapons to school and 10 percent reporting having been threatened with or injured by weapons at school. Over 25 percent of students had considered suicide and 10 percent had attempted suicide. Concerning drug use, findings showed that 53 percent had smoked cigarettes. High smoking rates were found among minorities, males, and older students. Over half had drunk alcohol, and 17 percent had used marijuana, with the percentage increasing by grade. Results concerning personal health revealed that about 25 percent consider themselves overweight but 40 percent are dieting, most of whom are females. Over 80 percent reported exercising or playing sports in the previous week in addition to attending physical education classes. Almost 80 percent reported AIDS education at school; 60 percent had discussed AIDS or HIV with parents or other family adults.

Resnick, M. D., Bearman, P. S., Blum, R. W., Bauman, K. E., Harris, K. M., Jones, J., Tabor, J., Beuhring, T., Sieving, R. E., Shew, M., Ireland, M., Bearinger, L. H., & Udry, J. R. (1997). Protecting adolescents from harm. Findings from the National Longitudinal Study on Adolescent Health. *Journal of the American Medical Association, 278,* 823-832.

The objective of this study was to identify risk and protective factors at the family, school, and individual levels as they relate to four domains of adolescent health and morbidity: emotional health, violence, substance use, and sexuality. The research design consisted of a cross-sectional analysis of interview data from the National Longitudinal Study of Adolescent Health. A total of 12,118 adolescents in grades 7 through 12 were drawn from an initial national school survey of 90,118 adolescents from 80 high schools plus their feeder middle schools. Eight areas were assessed: emotional distress; suicidal thoughts and behaviors; violence; use of three substances (cigarettes, alcohol, marijuana); and two types of sexual behaviors (age of sexual debut and pregnancy history). Independent variables included measures of family context, school context, and individual characteristics. Family and school contexts as well as individual characteristics are associated with health and risky behaviors in adolescents. The results should assist health and social service providers, educators, and others in taking the first steps to diminish risk factors and enhance protective factors for our young people.

Rumberger, R. W. (1995). Dropping out of middle school: A multilevel analysis of students and schools. *American Educational Research Journal, 32* (3), 583-625.

Using data from the 1988 National Educational Longitudinal Surveys (NELS) and hierarchical linear modeling (HLM), this study focuses on dropouts from middle school and examines the issue from both individual and institutional perspectives. Data for the study were drawn from the sample of 17,424 base-year students who were resurveyed in 1990. The final school sample consisted of 981 schools. At the individual level, the results identified a number of family and school experience factors that influence the decision to leave school, with grade retention being the single most powerful predictor. Additionally, there are widespread differences in the effects of these factors on White, Black, and Hispanic students. At the school level, the results revealed that average dropout rates vary widely between schools and that most of the variation can be explained by differences in the background characteristics of the students.

## Recommended Resources

Bosworth, K. (Ed.). (1999). *Preventing school violence: What schools can do.* Bloomington, IN: Phi Delta Kappa International.

Collaborative for Academic, Social, and Emotional Learning. (2003). *Safe and sound: An educational leader's guide to evidence-based social and emotional (SEL) programs.* Retrieved July 24, 2003, from http://www.casel.org/safeandsound.htm

Hoy, W. K., & Sabo, D. J. (1998). *Quality middle schools: Open and healthy.* Thousand Oaks, CA: Corwin Press.

Marx, E., Wooley, S. F., & Northrop, D. (Eds.) (1998). *Health is academic: A guide to coordinated school health programs.* New York: Teachers College Press.

McCarthy, A. R. (2000). *Healthy teens: Facing the challenges of young lives.* Birmingham, MI: Bridge Communications.

Wisconsin Department of Public Instruction. (1997). *Component quality: A comprehensive school health program assessment tool.* Madison, WI: Author.

## 6. MULTIFACETED GUIDANCE AND SUPPORT SERVICES.

### Research Summary

While research points to positive results of advisory programs (Connors, 1991; Mac Iver, 1990; Putbrese, 1989), such programs remain one of the most difficult middle level concepts to implement (Fenwick, 1992; Lounsbury & Clark, 1990). Many advisory programs are not functioning as they were initially intended and have simply taken the place of homeroom or have been abandoned.

Beane and Lipka (1987) presented the following description of advisory programs:

> Advisory programs are designed to deal directly with the affective needs of transescents. Activities may range from nonformal interactions to the use of systematically developed units whose organizing centers are drawn from the common problems, needs, interests, or concerns of transescents, such as "getting along with peers," "living in the school," or "developing self-concept." In the best of these programs, transescents have an opportunity to get to know one adult really well, to find a point of security in the institution, and to learn about what it means to be a healthy human being. (p. 40)

While there is still a need for considerably more research about the effectiveness of advisory programs (Clark & Clark, 1994), some of the most frequently mentioned purposes of advisories include:

(1) Promoting opportunities for social development
(2) Assisting students with academic problems
(3) Facilitating positive involvement among teachers, administrators, and students
(4) Providing an adult advocate for each student in the school
(5) Promoting positive school climate. (pp. 135-136)

Regarding the effectiveness of such programs, Mac Iver (1990) found that when teacher advisories focused on social and academic support activities, then a strong relationship existed that promoted the reduction of dropouts. Connors (1986) found evidence that advisory programs helped students grow emotionally and socially, contributed to a positive school climate, helped students learn about school and getting along with their classmates, and enhanced teacher-student relationships. George and Oldaker (1985) suggest that when advisory programs are combined with other components of the middle school concept, student self-concept improves, dropout rates decrease, and school climate becomes more positive.

While these studies all point to possible positive effects of advisory programs, we are warned that schools have a very difficult time implementing and sustaining this component of middle school reform (Fenwick, 1992; Lounsbury & Clark, 1990). A number of studies (Batsell, 1995; Bunte, 1995; Dale, 1993; Lee, 1995; Mosidi, 1994) addressed the implementation of advisory programs. Findings from this research document that successful implementation must address issues related to staff capacity, technical/administrative support, limits on the number of students (15-20) in each advisory, differing expectations on the part of teachers and administrators, the allotment of time to advisory periods as well as to teacher planning, a well-defined advisory curriculum, a feedback/maintenance loop for program review and revision, the transformation of the school's cultural norms, and the management of organizational politics.

Despite an expanding amount of literature on advisory programs, few researchers have systematically probed the subjective experiences of participants in advisory programs as disclosed by students and teachers. Sardo-Brown and Shetlar (1994) acknowledged that "more investigations of both teacher and student perceptions of the advisor-advisee periods need to be done in a variety of different types of schools" (p. 23). To this end, Anfara and Brown (Anfara & Brown, 2001; Brown & Anfara, 2001) conducted qualitative research that explores the perspectives of teachers. Teachers reported that "caring was women's work," that "battle lines" were drawn when administrators withdrew or withheld the necessary support from advisory teachers, and that a fine line exists between "mingling and meddling" in the lives of young adolescents.

## References Cited

Anfara, V. A., Jr., & Brown, K. (2001). Advisor-advisee programs: Community building in a state of affective disorder. In V. A. Anfara, Jr. (Ed.), *The handbook of research in middle level education* (pp. 3-34). Greenwich, CT: Information Age Publishing.

Batsell, G. (1995). *Progress toward implementation of developmentally responsive practice in middle level schools, 1989-1994.* Unpublished doctoral dissertation, University of Arizona.

Beane, J., & Lipka, R. (1987). *When the kids come first: Enhancing self-esteem.* Columbus, OH: National Middle School Association.

Bunte, A. (1995). *Success factors in the implementation of advisory programs in selected Illinois middle schools.* Unpublished doctoral dissertation, Southern Illinois University at Carbondale.

Brown, K., & Anfara, V. A., Jr. (2001). Competing perspectives on advisory programs: Mingling or meddling in middle schools. *Research in Middle Level Education Annual, 24,* 1-33.

Clark, S., & Clark, D. (1994). *Restructuring the middle level school: Implications for school leaders.* Albany, NY: State University of New York Press.

Connors, N. (1986). *A case study to determine the essential components and effects of an advisor/advisee program in an exemplary middle school.* Unpublished doctoral dissertation, Florida State University, Tallahassee, FL.

Connors, N. (1991). Teacher advisory: The fourth r. In J. L. Irvin (Ed.), *Transforming middle level education: Perspectives and possibilities* (pp. 162-178). Needham Heights, MA: Allyn and Bacon.

Dale, P. (1993). *Leadership, development, and organization of an advisory/advisee program: A comparative case study of two middle schools.* Unpublished doctoral dissertation, Fordham University, New York.

Fenwick, J. (1992). *Managing middle grade reform – An "American 2000" agenda.* San Diego, CA: Fenwick and Associates.

George, P., & Oldaker, L. (1985). *Evidence for middle school teaching.* Glenview, IL: Scott, Foresman and Company.

Lee, S. (1995). *Implementing the teacher advisory program at the middle school: A case study of technical, normative and political perspectives of change.* Unpublished doctoral dissertation, University of California, Los Angeles.

Lounsbury, J., & Clark, D. (1990). *Inside grade eight: From apathy to excitement.* Reston, VA: National Association of Secondary School Principals.

Mac Iver, D. (1990). Meeting the needs of young adolescents: Advisory groups, interdisciplinary teaching teams, and school transition programs. *Phi Delta Kappan, 71*(6), 458-464.

Mosidi, M. (1994). *A qualitative study of the process of implementing the advisor-advisee program in a school setting.* Unpublished doctoral dissertation, The University of Toledo.

Putbrese, L. (1989). Advisory programs at the middle level: The students' response. *NASSP Bulletin, 73*(514), 111-115.

Sardo-Brown, D., & Shetlar, J. (1994). Listening to students and teachers to revise a rural advisory program. *Middle School Journal, 26*(1), 23-25.

## Annotated References

Ayres, L.R. (1994). Middle school advisory programs: Findings from the field. *Middle School Journal, 25*(3), 8-14.

Although middle school students benefit greatly from well-planned, effectively delivered advisory programs, teachers remain uncommitted because of inadequate preparation, fear, and lack of experience. Subject-centered teachers often fear dealing with students in the affective domain. This article presents sample program development, staff development, and parent education plans underlying sound advisory systems.

Cole, C. (1992). *Nurturing a teacher advisory program.* Columbus, OH: National Middle School Association.

In recognition of the importance of effective advisory programs at the middle level, this monograph provides specific suggestions for organizing and sustaining a teacher advisory program and presents sample activities to assist program implementation. The first section of the book reviews aspects of early adolescent development that make an effective advisory program essential, while the second section suggests key program elements. Section three examines the roles of advisors, counselors, administrators, community members, and students in the whole advisory endeavor, while section four reviews the important characteristics and qualities of advisors. The fifth section addresses the development of advisory skills, including asking open-ended questions, restating students' comments, and using silence. The final sections of the book describe and suggest sources for successful activities, discuss administrative considerations, and suggest ways to involve parents and community members.

Galassi, J., Gulledge, S., & Cox, N. (1997). Middle school advisories: Retrospect and prospect. *Review of Educational Research, 67*(3), 301-338.

This article presents a critical analysis of middle school advisor-advisee programs and a review of the history and rationale for these programs. A typology is offered for distinguishing different advisory programs and a conceptual framework for identifying potential barriers to advisories at the inception as well as the implementation and maintenance phases. Suggestions for addressing these barriers are discussed. Guidelines for improving future research on advisories are presented. Finally, alternative educational practices for achieving the goals of advisory programs are considered.

James, M., & Spradling, N. (2001). *From advisory to advocacy: Meeting every student's needs.* Westerville, OH: National Middle School Association.

No longer just a separate program during a specified part of the school day, advocacy should permeate every minute and every activity. Advocacy refers to the conscious, ongoing relationship of every adult to every student. In this book, the authors provide a compelling rationale for student advocacy, list its implications and challenges, and provide specific activities for considering such a change. If your school is revamping an existing advisory program or thinking about starting one, this book is an important read.

Ziegler, S., & Mulhall, L. (1994). Establishing and evaluating a successful advisory program in a middle school. *Middle School Journal, 25*(4), 42-46.

Ziegler and Mulhall describe a principal-initiated advisory program at a Toronto middle school. Successful program elements are summarized, including a six-month planning period; a staff-supported inservice program offering training in team-building and adolescent development; daily advisory group meetings, with a maximum of 15 students, who retain the same advisor until graduation; and a handbook of resource units.

### Recommended Resources

Burkhardt, R. M. (2001). Advisory: Advocacy for every student. In T. Erb (Ed.), *This we believe...And now we must act* (pp. 35-41). Westerville, OH: National Middle School Association.

Forte, I., & Schurr, S. (1997). *A to Z active learning: Advisory and affective education.* Nashville, TN: Incentive Publications.

Galassi, J. P., Gulledge, S. A., & Cox, N. D. (1998). *Advisory: Definitions, descriptions, decisions, directions.* Columbus, OH: National Middle School Association.

Hoversten, C., Doda, N., & Lounsbury, J. (1991). *Treasure chest: A teacher advisory source book.* Columbus, OH: National Middle School Association.

James, M., & Spradling, N. (2001). *From advisory to advocacy: Meeting every student's needs.* Westerville, OH: National Middle School Association.

MacLaury, S. (2002). *Student advisories in grades 5-12: A facilitator's guide.* Norwood, MA: Christopher-Gordon Publishers.

PART FOUR

# Courageous Leadership:
# Teachers and Administrators

This We Believe (National Middle School Association, 1995) recognized the need for specially prepared middle level teachers noting that "educators need specific preparation before they enter middle level classrooms and continuous professional development as they pursue their careers" (p. 14). This position was reaffirmed and strengthened in the 2003 edition, *This We Believe: Successful Schools for Young Adolescents*. Now, more than ever before, this specific preparation is necessary. Due to the state licensing of teachers, most middle level teachers are either elementary or secondary certified. Perhaps even more serious, rarely can one find a middle school administrator who has received specific university preparation for working in middle schools. In short, we have a well-designed reform initiative with few people properly prepared to take the lead. In this part we look at the courageous leadership needed by both teachers and administrators to create successful schools for young adolescents.

### Research Summary – Teachers

From the early days of the junior high school to the recent release of position statements on teacher preparation by the National Middle School Association (2002) and the National Forum to Accelerate Middle-Grades Reform (2002), there has been much discussion about quality middle level teachers (Carnegie Council on Adolescent Development, 1989; Douglas, 1920; Jackson &

Davis, 2000; McEwin & Dickinson, 1997; Scales & McEwin, 1994; Vars, 1998). In 1920, Koos claimed

> In spite of all the importance that may be ascribed to other features of the junior high school, the supreme place of properly qualified teachers and principals in effecting thoroughgoing reorganization cannot be gainsaid. It is perhaps generally conceded that if a staff meeting all desirable requirements may be secured, the remaining features necessary for reorganization will almost automatically follow. (p. 163)

Making sure that young adolescents are afforded teachers who are specifically prepared to teach them is, then, neither a new issue, nor a topic seldom discussed.

Nevertheless, the research on middle level teacher education has been limited to studies that investigated the status of teacher licensure in the states and the extent, but not the quality, of teacher certification programs (e.g., McEwin & Allen, 1983; McEwin & Dickinson, 1995; Scales & McEwin, 1994; Valentine & Mogar, 1992). Only recently have researchers begun to examine the connection between middle grades certified teachers and student success in school.

A review of the studies on the status of middle grades licensure and certification reveals a gradual increase in the number of states offering middle grades licensure, but confirms that fewer than half of the states require specific licensure to teach in the middle grades, and certification areas overlap significantly within states (Gaskill, 2002). These circumstances hinder the development of quality middle grades teacher education programs and ultimately limit the number of fully prepared middle grades teachers.

Yet, we know intuitively and are beginning to show through research that fully prepared middle grades teachers are critical to the academic success of their students. This proposition is supported by the work of Darling-Hammond (2000) and Darling-Hammond, Chung, and Frelow (2002). More specifically for middle grades educators, researchers at the Center for Prevention Research and Development (CPRD) have begun to provide support for the critical connection between appropriate teacher preparation programs and student achievement (Flowers, Mertens, & Mulhall, 1999; Mertens, Flowers, & Mulhall, 2002). Together these researchers indicate that teachers who participated in specialized middle grades teacher education programs and are teaching in schools that have teaming and high levels of common planning time are more likely to be involved in effective team and classroom practices. Subsequently those teachers have the potential to effect greater gains in student learning, as defined by student achievement scores (Mertens et al., 2002).

## References Cited

Carnegie Council on Adolescent Development. (1989). *Turning points: Preparing American youth for the 21st century.* New York: Carnegie Corporation.

Darling-Hammond, L. (2000). Teacher quality and student achievement: A review of state policy evidence. *Education Policy Analysis Archives, 8*(1). Retrieved July 24, 2003, from http://epaa.asu.edu/epaa/vol8.html

Darling-Hammond, L., Chung, R., & Frelow, F. (2002). Variation in teacher preparation: How well do different pathways prepare teachers to teach? *Journal of Teacher Education, 53*(4), 286-302.

Douglas, A. (1920). *The junior high school.* Bloomington, IL: National Study of Education.

Flowers, N., Mertens, S. B., & Mulhall, P. E. (1999). The impact of teaming: Five research-based outcomes of teaming. *Middle School Journal, 31*(2), 57-60.

Gaskill, P. E. (2002). Progress in the certification of middle level personnel. *Middle School Journal, 33*(5), 33-40.

Jackson, A. W., & Davis, G. A. (2000). *Turning points 2000: Educating adolescents in the 21st century.* New York, NY: Teachers College Press.

Koos, L. V. (1920). *The junior high school.* New York: Harcourt, Brace, and Howe.

McEwin, C. K., & Allen, M. G. (1983). *Middle level teacher certification: A national study.* Boone, NC: Appalachian State University.

McEwin, C. K., & Dickinson, T. S. (1995). *The professional preparation of middle level teachers: Profiles of successful programs.* Columbus, OH: National Middle School Association.

McEwin, C. K., & Dickinson, T. S. (1997). Middle level teacher preparation and licensure. In J. L. Irvin (Ed.), *What current research says to the middle level practitioner* (pp. 223-229). Columbus, OH: National Middle School Association.

Mertens, S. B., Flowers, N., & Mulhall, P. (2002). The relationship between middle-grades teacher certification and teaching practices. In V. A. Anfara, Jr. & S. L. Stacki (Eds.), *Middle school curriculum, instruction, and assessment* (pp. 119-138). Greenwich, CT: Information Age Publishing.

National Forum to Accelerate Middle-Grades Reform. (2002). *Teacher preparation, licensure, and recruitment.* Newton, MA: Author.

National Middle School Association (1995). *This we believe: Developmentally responsive middle level schools.* Columbus, OH: Author.

National Middle School Association. (2002). *Quality teachers must have content knowledge and know how to teach that knowledge to young adolescents.* Westerville, OH: National Middle School Association. Retrieved July 24, 2003, from http://nmsa.org/news/trusteestatement_qualityteachers.htm

National Middle School Association (2003). *This we believe: Successful schools for young adolescents.* Westerville, OH: Author.

Scales, P. C., & McEwin, C. K. (1994). *Growing pains: The making of America's middle school teachers.* Columbus, OH: National Middle School Association.

Valentine, J. W., & Mogar, D. (1992). Middle level certification: An encouraging evolution. *Middle School Journal, 24*(2), 36-43.

Vars, G. F. (1998). Gordon F. Vars: Early writings. In R. David (Ed.), *Moving forward from the past: Early writings and current reflections of middle school founders* (pp. 187-221). Columbus, OH & Pittsburgh, PA: National Middle School Association & Pennsylvania Middle School Association.

## Annotated References

Darling-Hammond, L. (2000). Teacher quality and student achievement: A review of state policy evidence. *Education Policy Analysis Archives, 8*(1). Retrieved September 17, 2002, from http://epaa.asu.edu/epaa/vol8n1/

This study triangulates data from a 50-state survey of policies, case study analyses of policymaking at the state level, and the National Assessment of Educational Progress (NAEP) in order to examine the way in which teacher qualifications and other school inputs are related to student achievement. Quantitative and qualitative analyses both indicate that teacher quality, where quality is defined as the percentage with full certification and a major in the field, is more related to increases in student achievement, specifically in reading and mathematics than teachers' education level – even when controlling for student poverty and language status.

Darling-Hammond, L., Chung, R., & Frelow, F. (2002). Variation in teacher preparation: How well do different pathways prepare teachers to teach? *Journal of Teacher Education, 53*(4), 286-302.

According to Darling-Hammond, Chung, and Frelow (2002), a strong relationship exists between beginning teachers' preparation (program type) and their confidence in self-described teaching abilities. The extent to which beginning teachers feel well-prepared when they entered teaching was significantly correlated with

- Their sense of teaching efficacy (abilities in disciplinary content and content pedagogy; ability to deal with ambiguity and change; progressive teaching methods and continual self-renewal of useful methodology)
- Their sense of responsibility for student learning (dedication to all students to achieve and show marked growth in all domains: intellectual, social, emotional, and physical)
- Their plans to remain in teaching (professional development and personal growth)

Flowers, N., Mertens, S. B., & Mulhall, P. E. (1999). The impact of teaming: Five research-based outcomes of teaming. *Middle School Journal, 31*(2), 57-60.

The study indicates that students had the largest gain on their standardized achievement scores when they were enrolled in middle schools where there was teaming at all grade levels and high levels of common planning time for teachers; the students had the lowest gains in achievement in schools where teaming did not occur.

Gaskill, P. E. (2002). Progress in the certification of middle level personnel. *Middle School Journal, 33*(5), 33-40.

To update the information available on the status of middle grades credentials and make comparisons to the Valentine and Mogar study of 1992, the researcher collected extensive data from various Web sites of state teacher preparation/certification officers and then validated the data through direct contact with each state's certification officer. Data were then analyzed and reported as descriptive statistics. The data indicate that while we have seen an increase (four percent of states in 1969 to 86 percent of states in 2000) in credentialing agencies offering certification in the middle grades, less than 50 percent (21) of all states require specific middle grades preparation.

Mertens, S. B., Flowers, N., & Mulhall, P. (2002). The relationship between middle-grades teacher certification and teaching practices. In V. A. Anfara, Jr. & S. L. Stacki (Eds.), *Middle school curriculum, instruction, and assessment* (pp. 119-138). Greenwich, CT: Information Age Publishing.

Through a quantitative (descriptive and inferential) analysis of self-report survey data from 2001 teachers in 134 schools engaged in the Michigan Middle Start initiative, these researchers concluded that middle grades and elementary certified teachers were more likely to engage in classroom practices that are effective in teaching young adolescents. Teachers in schools with teaming and high levels of common planning time, regardless of certification type, reported higher levels of effective team and classroom practices. Furthermore, in schools where teaming and high levels of common planning time were the norm, middle grades-certified faculty reported the highest levels of effective team and classroom practices.

### Recommended Resources

Hart, L. E. (1997). Multicultural issues in middle level teacher education. In J. L. Irvin (Ed.) *What current research says to the middle level practitioner* (pp. 231-239). Columbus, OH: National Middle School Association.

McEwin, C. K., & Dickinson, T. S. (2001). Educators committed to young adolescents. In T. O. Erb (Ed.), *This we believe . . . And now we must act* (pp. 11-19). Westerville, OH: National Middle School Association.

McEwin, C. K., Dickinson, T. S., & Smith, T. W. (2003). Why specialized preparation is critical. *Kappa Delta Pi Record, 39*(2), 58-61.

McEwin, C. K., Dickinson, T. S., & Jenkins, D. M. (2003). *America's middle schools in the new century: Status and progress.* Westerville, OH: National Middle School Association.

National Board for Professional Teaching Standards. (2001). *The standards/ summaries of the standards.* Retrieved July 24, 2003, from http://www.nbpts.org/standards

National Middle School Association/National Council for Accreditation of
    Teacher Education. (2001). *NMSA middle level teacher preparation stan-
    dards.* Retrieved July 24, 2003, from http://nmsa.org

## Research Summary – Administrators

High-performing middle schools have high-performing, learning-centered
leaders – principals and teachers – working collaboratively to enhance student learning (Blase & Blase, 1998; Clark & Clark, 1994; Jackson & Davis,
2000; Levine, 1991). The research also clearly identifies specific roles and
behaviors that principals undertake to create an effective middle level program. Hallinger and Murphy (1986) classified these roles and behaviors into
three categories: (1) defining the school mission by creating a shared vision
focused on learning, (2) managing the instructional program, and (3) promoting and enhancing the school learning climate. In a study of 75 middle
schools in Pennsylvania, O'Donnell (2003) found that student achievement
in both mathematics and reading was significantly higher in schools where
principals were perceived by their teachers to exhibit a holistic, integrated
approach to the behaviors associated with these categories.

Effective middle level principals work with others to create and ar-
ticulate a shared vision of success focused on the needs and characteristics
of young adolescents (Valentine, Clark, Hackmann, & Petzko, 2002). Erb
(2001) indicated that in order to create this learner-centered vision, middle
level principals must have a deep understanding of the unique needs and
characteristics of the middle level learner and have knowledge of programs
and practices used to promote learning. However, Petzko, Clark, Valentine,
and Heckmann (2002) found, in their study of over 1,400 middle level leaders, that this "knowledge is not as widespread among current principals" (p.
4) as it had been in the ten years previously. However, the study did find that
principals believe that their teachers have a much stronger knowledge base
relating to middle level practice than reported in previous studies and that
teacher knowledge was a critical component in the development of a shared
vision.

Why is a clearly articulated, shared vision important? In a major study conducted by the Southern Regional Education Board of over 1800 middle grade teachers in 60 schools in 14 states, Cooney, Moore, and Bottoms (2002) found a significant difference between high-performing and low-performing schools on the question of clarity of goals and mission. Over 50 percent of teachers from high-performing schools reported that their school goals were clear to them, while only 37 percent of teachers in the lowest-performing schools reported clarity of goals. Teachers in the high-performing schools also reported that their principals consulted with them on school-related matters and that they worked together to improve student achievement. Another major finding of this study was that high-achieving schools had a strong vision and a set of practices centered on creating high expectations for all students where failure was not an option. Creating a vision that is focused on high achievement for all students, centered on the needs of the individual student, and shared by teachers is the essence of effective middle level leadership.

Effective middle level principals employ a number of strategies to manage the instructional program. In his review of the instructional leadership research, Murphy (1989) found that principals of effective schools manage the instruction of students by promoting quality instruction, supervising and evaluating instruction, protecting instructional time, coordinating the curriculum, and monitoring student progress. In a study of over 800 teachers, Blase and Blase (1999) identified the following specific principal behaviors that promote quality instruction. Principals identified by their teachers as effective instructional leaders (1) openly talk with teachers about teaching and learning, (2) provide teachers with time and encouragement for peer connections, (3) empower teachers to make decisions about curriculum and student learning, (4) engage in the professional development of teachers that focuses on teaching and learning, and (5) talk with students and parents about student learning. These activities do not mean that the principal is in control but that he or she knows what is going on in the school related to teaching and learning and ensures that teachers are focused on what matters most. The most effective principals ensure that teachers are making the key decisions related to learning and that they have the skills, knowledge, and resources necessary to make effective learning-based decisions. Finally, numerous studies have found that principals of high-performing middle schools use data to improve school and classroom practice. They develop a data plan with teachers and engage in meaningful discussions with teachers, parents, and students about the meaning of the data as it relates to student learning (Cooney, Moore, & Bottoms, 2002; Murphy & Hallinger, 1989; Short, Short, & Brinson, 1998).

Middle level reform has shifted the predominant view of schools as bureaucratic organizations to that of schools as communities. In a community of learners, leadership and power are no longer concentrated at the principal's level but require a more collaboratively shared leadership model (Clark, & Clark, 1996; Valentine, Clark, Hackmann, & Petzko, 2002). Sweetland and Hoy (2002) found in their study of 86 New Jersey middle schools that collaborative decision making and teacher empowerment significantly correlated with higher levels of reading and mathematics achievement. In addition to student achievement, when principals meaningfully engage their teachers in collaborative decision making and create norms of collegiality, teacher and student self-esteem, motivation, and self and group efficacy increase (Hipp, 1997; Tarter, Sabo, & Hoy, 1995). Developing the typical structures of a middle level program (teams, advisory, and flexible schedules) is a necessary first step in establishing a community of learners. However, Clark and Clark (2002) noted that without other more personal issues being addressed a change in the culture of the school will not occur. Based on their review of the literature on middle level reform, they identify the following issues: having a commitment of the principal to share power; providing for time and training for shared decision making to occur; focusing decision making on critical issues of teaching and learning; moving beyond the principal's council so that all teachers feel involved; and involving parents in important decisions that impact their children and the school. Creating a climate where teachers and parents believe that they are actively involved in the decision-making process has a significant impact on teaching and learning and increases student performance on both academic and non-academic measures (Cooney, Moore, & Bottoms, 2002; Peterson, Marks, & Warren, 1996).

The research on leadership is becoming clearer. Middle schools work when principals, teachers, and parents work together to achieve a common vision and place a strong emphasis on student learning and creating a culture of caring and support.

## References Cited

Blase, J., & Blase, J. (1998). *Handbook of instructional leadership: How really good principals promote teaching and learning.* Thousand Oaks, CA: Corwin Press.

Blase, J., & Blase, J. (1999). Effective instructional leadership through the teachers' eyes. *The High School Magazine, 7*(1), 17-20.

Cooney, S., Moore, B., & Bottoms, G. (2002). Preparing all students for high school. *Principal, 81*(3), 40-41.

Clark, S. N., & Clark, D. C. (1994). *Restructuring the middle level school: Implications for school leaders.* Albany, NY: State University of New York Press.

Clark, S. N., & Clark, D. C. (1996). Building collaborative environments for successful middle school restructuring. *NASSP Bulletin, 80*(578), 1–16.

Clark, S. N., & Clark, D. C. (2002). Collaborative decision making: A promising but underused strategy for middle school improvement. *Middle School Journal 33*(4), 52-57.

Erb, T. O. (2001). *This we believe...And now we must act.* Westerville, OH: National Middle School Association.

Jackson, A. W., & Davis, G. A. (2000). *Turning points 2000: Educating adolescents in the 21st century.* New York: Teachers College Press.

Hallinger, P., & Murphy, J. (1986). The social context of effective schools. *American Journal of Education, 94*(3), 328-355.

Hipp, K. A. (1997). The impact of principals in sustaining middle school change. *Middle School Journal, 28*(5), 42-45.

Levine, D. (1991). Creating effective schools: Findings and implications from research and practice. *Phi Delta Kappan, 75*(5), 389-393.

Murphy, J. (1989). Principal instructional leadership. In P. Thurston & L. Lotto (Eds.), *Advances in educational leadership* (pp. 163-200). Greenwich, CT: JAI Press.

Murphy, J., & Hallinger, P. (1989). A new era in the professional development of school administrators: Lessons from emerging programs. *Journal of Educational Administration, 27*(2), 22-45.

O'Donnell, R. (2003). Middle level principals' instructional leadership behaviors and student achievement. *Dissertation Abstracts International, 63*(12), 4175A. (UMI No. 3073966)

Peterson, K. D., Marks, H. M., & Warren, V. D. (1996, April). *SBDM in restructured schools: Organizational conditions, pedagogy, and student learning.* Paper presented at the annual meeting of the American Educational Research Association, New York, NY.

Petzko, V. N., Clark, D. C., Valentine, J. W., & Heckmann, D. G. (2002). Leaders and leadership in middle schools. *NASSP Bulletin, 86*(631), 3-9.

Short, P., Short, R., & Brinson, K. (1998). *Information collection: The key to database decision making.* Larchmont, NY: Eye on Education.

Sweetland, S., & Hoy, W. K. (2000). School characteristics and educational outcomes: Toward an organizational model of student achievement in middle schools. *Educational Administration Quarterly, 36*(5), 703-729.

Tarter, C. J., Sabo, D., & Hoy, W. K. (1995). Middle school climate, faculty trust, and effectiveness: A path analysis. *Journal of Research and Development in Education, 29*(1), 41-49.

Valentine, J. W., Clark, D. C., Hackmann, D. G., & Petzko, V. N. (2002). *Leadership in middle level schools, Vol 1: A national study of middle level learners and school programs.* Reston, VA: National Association of Secondary School Principals.

## Annotated References

Keefer, J. W., & Jenkins, J. M. (1997). *Instruction and the learning environment.* Larchmont, NY: Eye on Education.

This book focuses on providing practical skills and knowledge for the improvement of instruction. Specific chapters focus on such topics as the learning environment, instructional models, scheduling, and student motivation. Each chapter presents a summary of the knowledge base, provides useful tools, and concludes with action steps for the school leader.

Lucas, S. E., & Valentine, J. W. (2002, April). *Transformational leadership: Principals, leadership teams, and school culture.* Paper presented at the annual meeting of the American Educational Research Association, New Orleans, LA.

This study of 12 middle schools identified the relationship among principal transformational leadership, school leadership, team transformational leadership, and school culture. The findings indicate that the principal is the primary source for identifying and articulating the vision, while leadership teams seem to be the primary source for providing intellectual stimulation and holding high expectations. The principal exerts the greatest influence on teacher collaboration and unity of purpose. These findings support the continued move for collaborative decision making and outline the importance of the role of leadership teams. A comprehensive review of the literature on leadership and collaboration is presented.

Leithwood, K. A., & Riehl, C. (2003). *What we know about successful school leadership.* Philadelphia, PA: Laboratory for Student Success, Temple University.

   This brief, prepared by the Task Force on Developing Research in Educational Leadership of Division A of the American Educational Research Association, presents a summary of well-documented understandings about leadership at the school building level. The document can serve as a guide to enhance dialogue with diverse audiences about leadership issues.

Scribner, J. P., Cockrell, K. S., Cockrell, D. H., & Valentine, J. W. (1999). Creating professional communities in schools through organizational learning: An evaluation of a school improvement process. *Educational Administration Quarterly, 35*(1), 130-160.

   This article presents an analysis of the potential for a school improvement process to foster professional community in three rural middle schools through the process of organizational learning. The findings of this qualitative case study demonstrate the tensions schools negotiate between bureaucracy and professional community and suggest that four organizational factors influence the establishment of professional community: principal leadership, organizational history, organizational priorities, and organization of teacher work. Recommendations are offered.

Sergiovanni, T. J. (1992). *Moral leadership: Getting to the heart of school improvement.* San Francisco: Jossey-Bass.

   Sergiovanni demonstrates how creating a new leadership focus – one with a moral dimension centered on purpose, values, and beliefs – can transform a school from an organization to a community of learners. He describes how true collegiality, based on shared work and common goals, leads to natural interdependence among teachers and principals. Throughout the book he develops a process to foster moral leadership in the schools.

### Recommended Resources

Brown, K. M., & Anfara, V. A., Jr. (2003). *From the desk of the middle school principal: Leadership responsive to the needs of young adolescents.* Lanham, MA: The Scarecrow Press.

Jackson, A. W., & Davis, G. A. (Eds.). (2002). *Turning points 2000: Educating adolescents in the 21st century: Study guide.* New York: Teachers College Press.

National Forum to Accelerate Middle-Grades Reform. (2002). *The vision for middle-grades reform and schools to watch: Module 1 – vision.* Newton, MA: Educational Development Center.

Pedigo, M. (2003). *Differentiating professional development: The principal's role* (Middle Level Leadership Series). Westerville, OH: National Middle School Association.

Senge, P., Cambron-McCabe, N., Lucas, T., Smith, B., Dutton, J., & Kleiner, A. (2000). *Schools that learn: A fifth discipline fieldbook for educators, parents, and everyone who cares about education.* New York: Doubleday/Currency.

Stack, C. (2003). *A passion for proof: Using data to accelerate student achievement* (Middle Level Leadership Series). Westerville, OH: National Middle School Association.

PART FIVE

# Directions For Future Research

Research findings are powerful tools that help form opinions and beliefs about middle level practices. That is why this companion document to *This We Believe: Successful Schools for Young Adolescents* (National Middle School Association, 2003) is so valuable. It is a critical resource for extending our purpose and mission at a time when obstacles appear monumental.

Today's best practices are built on sound research and decades of disciplined inquiry. Research affirms middle level education as a distinct, separate level of schooling worthy of its own ideas, philosophies, and strategies. Its practice provides opportunities for scholars and practitioners to apply this knowledge in daily practice. In order to more adequately plan for the future of middle level education we offer the following six recommendations to fortify the research base.

First, **we need more large-scale, longitudinal studies.** In light of national educational policies (e.g., No Child Left Behind Act of 2001), middle school research would benefit significantly from more large-scale, longitudinal studies. Such studies need to focus on the effects or impact of the middle school concept on student achievement. Student achievement *must* be broadly defined to include more than just state level standardized tests. The social-emotional development of young adolescents must be figured into the definition of achievement. But student achievement as measured by standardized tests must be included if we hope to influence local, state, and national educational policies. Such studies need to be large-scale in nature to generate the reliability necessary to influence policy. Large-scale studies also provide for better generalizability across different types of schools and bolster our ability to influence policy.

Second, **we need studies that combine quantitative and qualitative methodologies**. Future educational research needs to include research designs incorporating both quantitative and qualitative methodologies. Currently there are very few mixed-methods studies. Both methodologies have their strengths and weaknesses; however, combining the two methodologies into a single research design offers numerous benefits. Such benefits include better triangulation of data, quantity plus quality, and contextual data to help explain quantitative data. Large-scale quantitative studies provide reliability and generalizability but lack the kinds of deep contextual information gained only through such qualitative methods as interviews, observations, and case studies.

Third, **we need studies that examine more than one middle school reform recommendation, practice, or design element.** The majority of the middle level research has focused on individual aspects, principles, practices, components, or design elements. For example, there are numerous studies focused specifically on interdisciplinary teaming, advisory programs, school climate, curriculum and instruction, and parent involvement. While these studies are important and have contributed greatly to middle school reform efforts, we need more studies that examine multiple components and how they are interrelated to one another within a school. It is only through such studies that we will gain a better understanding of how the various reform components are related to one another and where we find the greatest benefit.

Fourth, **we need more studies that replicate previous methods and designs.** Few middle level researchers use the same designs to collect, analyze, and report findings. Replicating studies is a must to validate the research base.

Fifth, **we need to design and conduct more experimental studies** that employ randomization and controls. The U. S. Department of Education has made it clear that educational research should move in this direction. Irrespective of our beliefs relative to educational research and school accountability, we must be able to respond appropriately to issues and attacks that are levied against the middle school concept.

Sixth, **we need to create a national database**. As discussed in *R³=Research, Rhetoric, and Reality: A Study of Studies Addressing NMSA's 21st Century Research Agenda and This We Believe* (Hough, 2003), the research community should generate a national database to address key questions relative to *This We Believe: Successful Schools for Young Adolescents* (National Middle School Association, 2003). To this end, an NMSA-sponsored national Database Planning Team has already held a series of strategy sessions and hopes to design an approach to collect data from middle level schools throughout the nation. If successful, this effort would produce a large database that would allow researchers opportunities to examine a variety of questions, including but not limited to "Do middle schools work?"

### References Cited

Hough, D. L. (2003). *R³=Research, rhetoric, and reality: A study of studies addressing NMSA's 21st Century Research Agenda and This We Believe.* Westerville, OH: National Middle School Association.

National Middle School Association. (2003). *This we believe: Successful schools for young adolescents.* Westerville, OH: Author.

No Child Left Behind Act of 2001. Public Law 107-110, 2002.

# National Middle School Association

National Middle School Association, established in 1973, is the voice for professionals and others interested in the education and well-being of young adolescents. The association has grown rapidly and enrolls members in all 50 states, the Canadian provinces, and 42 other nations. In addition, 58 state, regional, and provincial middle school associations are official affiliates of NMSA.

NMSA is the only national association dedicated exclusively to the education, development, and growth of young adolescents. Membership is open to all. While middle level teachers and administrators make up the bulk of the membership, central office personnel, college and university faculty, state department officials, other professionals, parents, and lay citizens are members and active in supporting our single mission – improving the educational experiences of 10- to 15-year-olds. This open and diverse membership is a particular strength of NMSA's.

The association publishes *Middle School Journal,* the movement's premier professional journal; *Research in Middle Level Education Online; Middle Ground, the Magazine of Middle Level Education; Family Connection,* an online newsletter for families; *Classroom Connections,* a practical quarterly resource; and a series of research summaries.

A leading publisher of professional books and monographs in the field of middle level education, NMSA provides resources both for understanding and advancing various aspects of the middle school concept and for assisting classroom teachers in planning for instruction. More than 70 NMSA publications as well as selected titles published by other organizations are available through the resource catalog .

The association's highly acclaimed annual conference has drawn many thousands of registrants every fall. NMSA also sponsors many other professional development opportunities.

For information about NMSA and its many services, contact the association's headquarters office at 4151 Executive Parkway, Suite 300, Westerville, Ohio, 43081. TELEPHONE: 800-528-NMSA; FAX: 614-895-4750; INTERNET: www. nmsa.org.